SHEFFIELD'S MILITARY LEGACY

GERRY VAN TONDER

Pen & Sword
MILITARY

To my wife, Tracey

First published in Great Britain in 2017 by
PEN AND SWORD MILITARY
an imprint of
Pen and Sword Books Ltd
47 Church Street
Barnsley
South Yorkshire S70 2AS

Copyright © Gerry van Tonder, 2017

ISBN 978 1 52670 762 8

The right of Gerry van Tonder to be identified as the author of this work
has been asserted in accordance with the Copyright, Designs and Patents Act 1988.

Typeset by Aura Technology and Software Services, India
Maps, drawings and militaria in the colour section by Colonel Dudley Wall
Printed and bound in Malta by Gutenberg

Pen & Sword Books Ltd incorporates the imprints of Pen & Sword
Archaeology, Atlas, Aviation, Battleground, Discovery, Family History, History, Maritime, Military,
Naval, Politics, Railways, Select, Social History, Transport, True Crime, Claymore Press, Frontline
Books, Leo Cooper, Praetorian Press, Remember When, Seaforth Publishing and Wharncliffe.

For a complete list of Pen and Sword titles please contact
Pen and Sword Books Limited
47 Church Street, Barnsley, South Yorkshire, S70 2AS, England
email: enquiries@pen-and-sword.co.uk
website: www.pen-and-sword.co.uk

CONTENTS

Bronze of a First World War officer, York and Lancaster War Memorial, Weston Park. (Photo Gerry van Tonder)

INTRODUCTION

In the century following the Norman invasion, a castle was built at the confluence of the rivers Sheaf and Don, an early recognition of Sheffield's strategic importance. Destroyed in the thirteenth century during the Second Barons' War, a second castle was built on the site, but in 1647, it was ordered to be demolished immediately after the cessation of the Civil War, thereby negating any future tactical use by either Parliamentarian or Royalist.

Steel production and downstream manufacturing would, however, be perpetually embedded in the military legacy of this seat of industrial innovation and production.

The Vickers steel foundry was established in Sheffield in 1828. Following the manufacture of the factory's first artillery in 1890, Sheffield expanded to find itself a leading supplier in the First World War, feeding the military with ammunition shells, guns and cannons for ships, armour plating, aircraft parts, torpedoes, helmets and bayonets. Sheffield's major contribution to the British war machine in the Second World War quickly attracted the attention of Nazi Germany. In December 1940, in an operation appropriately codenamed *Schmelztiegel*, or Crucible, for the method of steel production, Sheffield suffered two major raids aimed primarily at steel and munitions factories.

A centuries-old proud tradition of answering a call to the colours spawned formation titles of courage and dedicated service – the 84th Regiment of Foot, the Loyal Independent Sheffield Volunteers of the 1700s, the Hallamshire Rifle Volunteers raised in 1859, and the Sheffield Squadron, Yeomanry Cavalry.

The 1899–1902 Anglo-Boer War would also have an enduring legacy on the town, as many volunteered to fight on the sub-continent. The Sheffield Wednesday football stadium was given the name Spioen Kop, after the famous battle in South Africa, while local road names include Ladysmith Avenue and Mafeking Place.

On 1 July 1916, the Sheffield City Battalion fought in a heroic and costly, but hopeless, action

Vickers-made and Barnes Wallis-designed 10-ton 'Grand Slam' bomb. (Photo Gerry van Tonder)

on the Somme to capture the village of Serre, and through the Second World War right up to Afghanistan, Sheffield's men and women in uniform were not found wanting.

Sheffield's rich military legacy portrayed in this publication is drawn from a cross section of representative units, home and foreign actions, uniformed personalities, barracks at the hub of musters, the calibre of gallantry – including six Victoria Crosses – as well as the immortality of names on memorials, such as the Sheffield Memorial Park in France.

The uniquely titled Hallamshires would, in the Second World War, ensure that Sheffield's military pride will, in perpetuity, be indelibly inscribed in the city's august legacy. Serving for the duration of their European campaign, the Hallamshires proudly wore the polar bear shoulder patch that identified them as members of the 49th Division. From the frozen Norwegian and Icelandic theatres to North-West Europe, where the battalion led the division across the Seine, the Dutch border and finally the Rhine as the war drew to a close.

The York and Lancaster Regiment elected to disband when the British army was reorganized in 1968, one of only two British regiments to do so. The colours were laid up for the last time in the regiment's own St George's Memorial Chapel in Sheffield Cathedral. In the hallowed surrounds of the chapel, the visitor is able to absorb the full tableau of the city's noble and honoured military endowment.

The 49th (West Riding) Infantry Division 'Polar Bear' Memorial, National Memorial Arboretum. (Photo Gerry van Tonder)

1. A BRIEF HISTORY

Up until the Norman conquest of 1066, Sheffield pertained more to an area successively occupied by Romans, Danes and Anglo-Saxons and characterized by several small settlements.

Shortly after the arrival of the Normans, a rudimentary wooden motte-and-bailey castle was erected at the confluence of the Sheaf and Don rivers. A market town developed around the stronghold. The construction of the castle is generally attributed to an Anglo-Norman baron from Huntingdonshire, William de Lovetot. Upon the marriage of his granddaughter, Maud, to Gerard de Furnival in 1204, ownership of the castle passed to the de Furnival family. It was when grandson Thomas was at the head of the family seat, that in 1266 the castle was razed to the ground by anti-royalist barons during the Second Barons' War of 1264–67. Thomas, as loyal supporter of the monarch, made Sheffield a target for a force of barons under John de Eyvill that was marching from north Lincolnshire to Derbyshire. De Eyvill put the castle and church to the torch and destroyed the settlement. In 1270, in return for his sacrifice, King Henry III granted Thomas a charter to build another castle. This time, stone was the principal building material.

By the start of the seventeenth century, Sheffield had already developed a reputation for the production of cutlery, growing to become the main producer of cutlery outside London.

From 1570 to 1584, Mary, Queen of Scots, was incarcerated in Sheffield Castle and Sheffield Manor.

The localized polarization of loyalties to either monarch or parliament characterized the first half of seventeenth-century Britain. Inevitably, armed conflict ensued, recorded in history as the Civil War. In October 1642, Parliamentarian Sir John Gell took Sheffield Castle on behalf of their cause. In April the following year, however, the Earl of Newcastle reclaimed the castle as a traditional Royalist strongpoint. Two years later, as the fortunes of the two belligerent camps continued to vacillate, a 1,200-strong Parliamentarian force under Major General Crawford, acting on behalf of the Earl of Manchester, resorted to the use of artillery to breach Sheffield Castle's walls, forcing the defenders to sue for peace. Under generous terms of conditional surrender, the Royalist occupants under Major Beaumont were granted safe passage out of the castle, allowing them to return home unhindered and without persecution.

As with other disputed castles that had provided strategic strongholds for rival forces, in 1647 Parliament promulgated that Sheffield Castle be levelled.

Around the 1740s, the crucible steel process of manufacturing was developed, resulting in a far better grade of steel. This proved to be a major innovative landmark in the industrialization of Sheffield.

The 2nd Battalion, 12th Regiment of Foot was raised in 1756, after separating from the 12th Suffolk Regiment, forming the basis of the 65th Regiment of Foot two years later.

Scythe grinding, Sheffield, 1860. (Wood engraving by M. Jackson)

In 1782, a county name was incorporated and the regiment retitled the 65th (2nd Yorkshire, North Riding) Regiment of Foot.

In November 1793, in response to events in France, the 84th Regiment of Foot was raised at York by Lieutenant Colonel George Bernard.

In May 1794, the Loyal Independent Sheffield Volunteers, was raised as a precaution against internal revolt and foreign invasion. In June of this year, Lord Fitzwilliam was appointed captain of the newly formed Rotherham Troop of Yeomanry Cavalry. In August, the Corps of Yorkshire West Riding Yeomanry Cavalry was divided into two regiments, each with five troops. The 1st, or Southern Regiment, West Yorkshire Yeomanry Cavalry, comprised a troop from each of Sheffield, Rotherham, Doncaster, Pontefract and Barnsley. Lieutenant Colonel Bryan Cooke was appointed colonel commandant. The Sheffield Troop grew to form a squadron made up of A and B troops. There were, at this time, also companies of voluntary 'supplementary militia'.

In 1808, a second battalion of the 84th was raised, and the regiment retitled the 84th (York and Lancaster) Regiment of Foot, in recognition of the two formation counties Yorkshire and Lancashire.

Following government's reluctant sanctioning of the raising of volunteer rifle corps, at a meeting that took place at Sheffield Town Hall on 26 May 1859, it was agreed to form a volunteer infantry unit out of concern that war with France was imminent. On 22 June, it was declared that the title Hallamshire Rifles would be 'suitable'. Retitled the Hallamshire Rifle

It would be a miracle indeed, if, during the present rage for Battle and Murder, certain inhabitants of Sheffield were outstripped in quixotic loyalty by any town in England. A number of heroes have accordingly agreed to form themselves into a Military Corps, to be called *The Independent Sheffield Volunteers*; to be armed, accoutred, clothed and disciplined at their own expence, with the charitable intention, we are told, of being ready, when *required*, to embue their hands in the blood of those of their fellow-town-men who are so audaciously rebellious as to – SPEAK AS THEY THINK!!!

In the afternoon of Thursday last, Mr. Peech, of the Angel Inn, in this place, accompanied with about half-a-score of his grey coach horses, a number of sergeants and recruits, and a drum and fife, paraded the streets, followed chiefly by a rabble of children, amidst shoutings, hootings and hissings, &c. The noise of the cavalcade, which was continued till the evening, as was natural, drew together a number of mechanics before the Angel Inn, who expressed their displeasure at the proceedings of this party; but at length, to the utter disappointment of certain persons, went home *peaceably*.

Sheffield Register, Yorkshire, Derbyshire,
& Nottinghamshire Universal Advertiser, Friday, 2 May 1794

Corps, a few months later a request to alter the title to the 2nd Yorkshire West Riding (Hallamshire) Rifle Volunteer Corps was officially granted.

Early in 1861, the Sheffield Artillery Volunteer Corps was formed, holding its first drill on 9 February. Captain Creswick, later lieutenant colonel, was appointed commander, and the unit titled the 4th West York Sheffield Artillery Volunteers. In June, the regiment was ceremoniously presented with the Town Guns, originally owned by the Sheffield Volunteers of 1803.

The Childers Reforms of 1881 saw the amalgamation of the 65th and 84th regiments of foot to form the York and Lancaster Regiment.

In December 1899, a nationwide appeal went out for volunteer troopers to serve with the Imperial Yeomanry in

3rd West Yorkshire Light Infantry officer's tunic, 1854. (Photo Gerry van Tonder)

the three-month-old war against the Boer republics in South Africa. A Sheffield contingent was raised, which, together with the York and Lancaster Regiment, saw active service in South Africa.

During the First World War, the York and Lancaster Regiment raised twenty-two battalions.

The line battalion of the 4th (Hallamshire) Territorial Battalion was headquartered in Sheffield in August 1914. Two reserve battalions of the 4th, the 2/4th and 3/4th, were formed in September 1914 and March 1915 respectively. In the order of battle on the Western Front, the 1/4th formed part of 148th Brigade, 49th (West Riding) Division. The 2/4th was with 187th Brigade, 62nd (2nd West Riding) Division. The 3/4th became the 4th Reserve Battalion, before absorbing the 5th (formerly 3/5th) Reserve Battalion to become the West Riding Reserve Brigade.

Recruitment for the 'Sheffield University and City Special Battalion' commenced on 5 September 1914 at enlistment stations throughout the city, including Town Hall, resulting in the formation the 12th (Service) Battalion Sheffield. In France, the battalion joined 94th Brigade, 31st Division VIII Corps, Fourth Army.

On the first day of the Battle of the Somme, 1 July 1916, the City Battalion, as it became known, suffered catastrophic casualties at Serre, France. The 12th was disbanded in France on 17 February 1918.

Sheffield and Rotherham, the giants of Britain's steel industry, became essential elements of the nation's war machine at this time, producing shells and guns for the Royal

Troops of the 49th Division near Maillly Maillet, November 1916. (Photo Ernest Brooks)

Navy, in addition to armour plate and parts for aircraft and torpedoes. Vickers, founded in Sheffield in 1828, produced the iconic machine gun by the thousands. Smaller items such as helmets, bayonets and body armour were also manufactured in the city's versatile mills.

In October 1939, the 1st Battalion, York and Lancaster Regiment was deployed to France to join 15th Brigade, 5th Infantry Division. After evacuation back to Britain, the battalion went on to serve in the Middle East and the Allied invasion of Sicily and Italy. From here, they participated in the invasion of Nazi Germany.

The 2nd Battalion, after the Battle of Crete, joined the 70th Infantry in North Africa, sustaining heavy casualties during the breakout from Tobruk. From here, the battalion was deployed to India and Burma.

The 4th (Hallamshire) Battalion, as part of 146th Infantry Brigade, 49th (West Riding) Infantry Division, were deployed to Norway and Iceland, before returning to the UK in April 1942. The battalion took part in the Normandy Invasion in June 1944, fighting through Europe to play an active role in the liberation of Arnhem in April 1945.

In 1936, the 5th Battalion (Territorial Army) became the 67th (York and Lancaster) Heavy Anti-Aircraft Regiment, seeing active service in North Africa, India and Burma.

The 6th Battalion was a territorial second line of the 4th Battalion. Posted to 138th Infantry Brigade, 46th Infantry Division, the 6th was part of the British Expeditionary Force evacuated from Dunkirk in June 1940. The battalion then saw service in French North Africa, and the Allied invasion of Italy in September 1943.

Raised in 1940, the 7th Battalion served on the North-West Frontier, before being posted to Burma towards the end of the war.

Also raised in 1940, the 8th and 9th battalions were deployed to Northern Ireland with 71st Brigade, before being sent to India to form part of the 25th Indian Infantry Division – the 8th with the 51st Indian Infantry Brigade and the 9th with the 53rd Indian Infantry Brigade. The two sister battalions saw action in the Arakan, Malaya, and in southern Burma.

While in India, the 10th Battalion converted to armour and was retitled the 150th Regiment, Royal Armoured Corps. As part of the 254th Indian Tank Brigade, the 150th was issued with American-made M3 Lee tanks, participating in the Indian and Burma campaigns, including the advance on Rangoon.

The Second World War provided a lifeline for the 1930s flagging steel industries in Sheffield. This included Vickers, which manufactured crankshafts for Rolls-Royce Merlin engines and Hadfield's who manufactured 18in. armour-piercing shells. Vickers also manufactured the massive Barnes Wallis-designed 10-ton 'earthquake' bomb, called the Grand Slam. The city continued to mill steel for ships, aircraft and tanks.

This made Sheffield a target for the Luftwaffe. In mid-December 1940, 660 people perished and 80,000 buildings were destroyed in three days of heavy bombing raids over the city.

In August 1939, an RAF station opened at Lightwood, three miles from the Sheffield city centre. This site became home to No. 16 Balloon Centre, part of No. 33 (Barrage Balloon) Group, RAF. The centre was made up of 939 (West Riding) (Sheffield West),

M3 Lee tank. (Photo US NARA)

940 (West Riding) (Rotherham) and 941 (West Riding) (Sheffield Central) squadrons. Each squadron had three flights of eight balloons each. In August 1940, 941 Squadron was disbanded due to a lack of volunteers, its equipment and personnel transferred to 939 Squadron. The centre had responsibility for seventy-two barrage balloons for the aerial defence of Sheffield. In 1943, the centre was renamed RAF Norton.

From May and December 1943, Norton was a sub-site for 35 Maintenance Unit, and again from October 1951 to February 1953. RAF Norton was also home to the Aircrew Refresher School from July 1943 to July 1945, a disciplinary centre for members of the RAF who had breached the air force's codes of conduct.

As the Luftwaffe threat had tailed off significantly by 1943–44, most of the balloons were translocated to be deployed over London. The centre was shut down towards the end of 1944.

After the war, No. 3 Ground Radar Servicing Section took up occupation as a school, under the command of 90 (Signals) Group. As an RAF station, Norton closed in January 1965.

After the Second World War, the York and Lancaster Regiment was stationed in various parts of the world, seeing active service in the Korean War, Suez Crisis and Malayan Emergency.

With the reorganization of the British army, the defence review of 1968, the regiment was one of only two in Britain that chose disbandment over amalgamation with other regiments. The Yorkshire Volunteers, a legacy of the 4th (Hallamshire) Battalion, was formed in April 1967 as an infantry regiment of the British territorial army. The 4th and 5th Battalions – the Green Howards – together with four other Yorkshire battalions, merged into the new regiment, with one company based in Sheffield. All five constituent battalions were then reduced to cadre status.

In 1971, the 2nd and 3rd battalions were raised by the five infantry cadres and the three Yorkshire-based territorial army Royal Artillery regiments. Of these, the 3rd Battalion Yorkshire Volunteers and the Sheffield Artillery Volunteers amalgamated to form B Battery, 3rd Battalion, Yorkshire Volunteers.

After a short independent existence of only four years, in 1992, the 4th Battalion was merged with the 3rd, its headquarters in Sheffield. Following a further defence review, the whole regiment was broken up and recreated as three battalions of three Yorkshire infantry regiments. The 1st Battalion became 4th/5th Battalion Green Howards (Yorkshire Volunteers), 2nd Battalion became 3rd Battalion, The Prince of Wales's Own Regiment of Yorkshire (Yorkshire Volunteers), and 3rd/4th Battalion became 3rd Battalion, The Duke of Wellington's Regiment (West Riding) (Yorkshire Volunteers).

On 16 December 2006, the three regiments officially merged to form the Yorkshire Regiment – Yorkshire Warriors – and the Yorkshire Volunteers was assigned to history. The new regiment, with the motto 'Fortune Favours the Brave', comprises 1st Battalion, the Yorkshire Regiment (Prince of Wales's Own) (formerly 1st Battalion, Prince of Wales's Own Regiment of Yorkshire), 2nd Battalion, the Yorkshire Regiment (Green Howards) (formerly 1st Battalion, Green Howards), 3rd Battalion, the Yorkshire Regiment (Duke of Wellington's) (formerly 1st Battalion, the Duke of Wellington's Regiment (West Riding), and 4th Battalion,

1st Battalion, the Yorkshire Regiment soldier on patrol in Afghanistan (Photo MoD)

the Yorkshire Regiment (formerly Prince of Wales's Own company of The East and West Riding Regiment, Green Howards company from the Tyne-Tees Regiment and two companies of The Duke of Wellington's Regiment from The East and West Riding Regiment).

The regiment's first major operational tour of duty was as 1 YORKS (Prince of Wales's Own) Battle Group to Basra, Iraq, in November 2006, in which A, B and C companies were deployed.

The 2nd Battalion (Green Howards) was deployed to Helmand Province, Afghanistan, for a period of six months in September 2007 in a mentoring and liaison role with the Afghan National Army.

In 2008, B Company Group of 1st Battalion (Prince of Wales's Own) was deployed to Kosovo for six months on Operation Oculus (K) as the last British Intelligence, Surveillance & Reconnaissance Task Force (ISR TF).

In November that year, a contingent from the 1st Battalion (Prince of Wales's Own) was redeployed to Iraq on Operation Telic 13. In May the following year, A Company of the 1st transferred their British military HQ protection duties in Baghdad, to Alma Company of the 3rd Battalion (Duke of Wellington's). Alma Company was among the last British soldiers to leave Iraq in July 2009.

More than ninety troops from the 3rd Battalion (Duke of Wellington's) were deployed to Helmand Province in August 2009 as 'battle casualty replacements' to other British regiments in the province. Burma Company of the 3rd Battalion (Duke of Wellington's) deployed to Afghanistan in the same year, followed by elements of Corunna Company. In September, the 2nd Battalion (Green Howards), with sixty troops of the 4th Battalion, was deployed for seven months with 11th Light Brigade in Operation Herrick XI as the OMLT (Operational Mentoring and Liaison Team) Battle Group.

In a first for the 1st Battalion (Prince of Wales Own), in October 2011, the whole battalion was deployed to Helmand Province for a six-month tour of duty in support of

TROUBLE IN AFGHANISTAN

The news that there has been a rising in the north of Afghan Turkestan is vague and unconfirmed, but is not improbable.

Risings are always as probable in Afghanistan as by-elections in England. The seizure of Khanibad, if true, is, however, a serious misfortune for the Ameer. Khanibad is his Midlothian, and its capture by a rebel would be worse than the return of a Tory candidate for Edinburghshire.

The rebel Khan will probably have his throat cut before many weeks are over; but of course there is a chance that the rising may spread. That is only another reason for deploring the lamentable policy of procrastination by which Lord Granville has left the Afghan frontier unsettled to this hour.

Luton Times and Advertiser, Tuesday, 3 July 1855

the 20th Armoured Brigade. A Company was attached to the 3rd Battalion the Royal Regiment of Scotland, and B and C companies with the Danish army. Together with the 1st Queen's Dragoon Guards, 1st Battalion formed the Brigade Reconnaissance Force.

In April 2012, the 3rd Battalion relieved the 5th Battalion, The Rifles, at Nahr-e Saraj (South) in Helmand Province.

While on a training exercise in Kenya in February 2013, sixteen troops from the 1st Battalion (Prince of Wales's Own) reconnaissance platoon staged a mutiny. Led by an NCO, the troops refused to obey commands, saying that their new commanding officers were incompetent 'muppets' who consumed excessive amounts of alcohol. Found guilty, but with extenuating circumstances, none was discharged, but sentenced to forty to sixty days' military imprisonment.

The Yorkshire Regiment was reduced to two regular battalions in January 2013. The 1st and 3rd battalions absorbed the 2nd Battalion, out of which the 1st and 2nd battalions, the Yorkshire Regiment emerged. For the first time, historic regimental titles were discarded.

In October 2014, Britain announced that a small number of troops from the Yorkshire Regiment's 2nd Battalion were training Kurdish forces in the use of British-supplied heavy machine guns in their fight against so-called Islamic State (IS) militants.

The only remaining regimental presence in Sheffield is a company of the 4th Battalion – referred to as 4 YORKS – operating from an army reserve centre in the city.

The Sheffield University Officers' Training Corps (SUOTC), functioning under the Yorkshire Officers' Training Regiment, is today one the largest officer training corps in the UK. Attracting students from universities across Yorkshire, including, specifically, the University of Sheffield and Sheffield Hallam University, the institution is located at Somme Barracks in the Sheffield city centre.

The Yorkshire Regiment battle honours listed here include all those earned by the antecedent regiments throughout its history. For ease of identification, the conflict in which battle honours were earned is also shown:

Namur 1695 (Nine Years' War)
Blenheim, Ramillies, Oudenaarde, Malplaquet (War of the Spanish Succession)
Louisburg, Dettingen (War of the Austrian Succession)
Quebec 1759, Martinique 1762, Havannah (Seven Years' War)
St Lucia 1778, Martinique 1794 and 1809 (American War of Independence)
Tournay, Belle Isle (War of the First Coalition)
Hindoostan, Mysore, Ally Ghur, Delhi 1803, Leswaree, Deig (Second Anglo-Maratha War)
Seringapatam (Fourth Anglo-Mysore War)
Corunna, Nive, Peninsula, Guadelupe 1810, Waterloo (Napoleonic Wars)
Siege of Bhurtpore 1825–26 (Jat War 1825–26)
Alma, Inkerman, Sevastopol, Abyssinia (Crimean War)
New Zealand (New Zealand War)
Tirah, Afghanistan 1879–80 (Second Anglo-Afghan War)
Relief of Ladysmith, Relief of Kimberley, Paardeberg, South Africa 1900–02 (Anglo-Boer War)

Protected-vehicle patrol, Afghanistan. (Photo MoD)

First World War:
Mons, Le Cateau, Retreat from Mons, Battle of the Marne 1914 and 1918, Aisne 1914 and 1918, Armentières 1914, La Bassée 1914, Ypres 1914, 1915, 1917 and 1918, Langemarck 1914 and 1917, Gheluvelt, Nonne Bosschen, Neuve Chapelle, Hill 60, Gravenstafel, St Julien, Frezenberg, Bellewaarde, Aubers, Festubert, Hooge 1915, Loos, Somme 1916 and 1918, Albert 1916 and 1918, Bazentin, Delville Wood, Pozières, Flers-Courcelette, Morval, Thiepval, Le Transloy, Ancre Heights, Ancre 1916, Arras 1916, 1917 and 1918, Scarpe 1917 and 1918, Arleux, Oppy, Bullecourt, Hill 70, Messines 1917 and 1918, Pilckem, Menin Road, Polygon Wood, Broodseinde, Poelcappelle, Passchendaele, Cambrai 1917 and 1918, St Quentin, Bapaume 1918, Rosières, Ancre 1918, Villiers Bretonneux, Lys, Estaires, Hazebrouck, Bailleul, Kemmel, Bethune, Scherpenberg, Marne 1918, Tardenois, Amiens, Drocourt-Quéant, Hindenburg Line, Havrincourt, Épéhy, Canal du Nord, St Quentin Canal, Beaurevoir, Selle, Valenciennes, Sambre, France and Flanders 1914–18, Piave, Vittorio Veneto, Italy 1917–18, Struma, Doiran 1917, Macedonia 1915–18, Suvla, Landing at Suvla, Scimitar Hill, Gallipoli 1915, Egypt 1915–1916, Archangel 1918.

Afghanistan 1919 (Third Anglo-Afghan War)

Second World War:
Otta, Norway 1940, Withdrawal to Escaut, Defence of Arras, French Frontier 1940, Ypres-Comines Canal, Dunkirk 1940, St. Valery-en-Caux, Normandy Landing, Tilly sur Seulles, Odon, Fontenay Le Pesnil, Caen, Bourguebus Ridge, Troarn, Mont Pincon, St Pierre La Vielle, Gheel, Nederrijn, Aam, Venraij, Rhineland, Schaddenhof, Brinkum, Bremen, North-West Europe 1940 and 1944–45, Jebel Defeis, Keren, Ad Teclescan, Abyssinia 1940–41, Gazala, Cauldron, Mersa Matruh, Defence of Alamein Line, El Alamein, Mareth, Wadi ZigZaou, Akarit, North Africa 1940–42, 1942–43 and 1943, Banana Ridge, Medjez Plain, Gueriat el Atach Ridge, Tunis, Djebel Bou Aoukaz 1943, North Africa 1943, Primasole Bridge, Landing in Sicily, Lentini, Sicily 1943, Minturno, Anzio, Campoleone, Rome, Monte Ceco, Italy 1943–44 and 43–45, Sittang 1942, Pegu 1942, Paungde, Yenangyaung 1942, North Arakan, Maungdaw, Defence of Sinzweya, Imphal, Bishenpur, Kanglantonbi, Kohima, Meiktila, Capture of Meiktila, Defence of Meiktila, Rangoon Road, Pyawbwe, Arakan beaches, Chindits 1944, Burma Campaign (1942–44).

The Hook 1953, Korean War 1952–53 (Korean War)
Iraq 2003 (Iraq War)

British infantry regiments are restricted as to the number of battle honours that may be displayed on the Queen's and Regimental colours. On the Queen's Colour, the maximum is 43 from the two world wars, while on the Regimental Colour it is 46 from other conflicts.

At amalgamation, the Yorkshire Regiment had to select battle honours from the full list to display on its new colours. This was the final selection:

Queen's Colour:
Mons; Marne 1914, 18; Aisne 1914, 18; Armentieres 1914; Ypres 1914, 15, 17, 18; Hill 60; Loos; Somme 1916, 18; Arras 1917, 18; Cambrai 1917, 18; Lys; Tardenois; Selle; Valenciennes; Piave; Vittoria Veneto; Doiran 1917; Suvla; Gallipoli 1915; Norway 1940; Dunkirk; St Valery en Caux; Normandy Landing; Odon; Fontenay le Pesnil; Schaddenhof; NW Europe 1940, 44–45; Keren; Gazala; El Alamein; Mareth; Akarit; Djebel Bou Aoukaz 1943; Sicily 1943; Minturno; Anzio; Monte Ceco; Sittang 1942, 45; Pegu 1942; Defence of Sinweya; Imphal; Meiktila; Burma 1942–45.

Regimental Colour:
Namur 1695; Blenheim; Ramillies; Oudenaarde; Malplaquet; Dettingen; Louisburg; Quebec 1759; Bell isle; Martinique 1762; Havannah; St Lucia 1778; Martinique 1794, 1809; Tournay; Mysore; Seringapatam; Ally Ghur; Delhi 1803; Leswaree; Deig; Corunna; Guadeloupe 1810; Java; Nive; Peninsula; Waterloo; Bhurtpore; Alma; Inkerman; Sevastopol; New Zealand; Abyssinia; Afghanistan 1879–80; Tirah; Relief of Kimberley; Paardeberg; Relief of Ladysmith; South Africa 1899–1902; Afghanistan 1919; Korea 1952–53; The Hook 1953; Iraq 2003.

In addition to these battle honours, the regimental colour also displays four emblems from the preceding regiments:

Top right: White Horse of Hanover, the Prince of Wales's Own Regiment of Yorkshire.
Bottom left: Star of Brunswick, the Prince of Wales's Own Regiment of Yorkshire.
Bottom right: Dannebrog Cross, the Green Howards.
Bottom centre: Elephant and Howdah, the Duke of Wellington's Regiment

The battalion's Roman numeral is in the top left corner of each flag. The use of the Cross of St George as the background is unique to the Yorkshire Regiment.

2. CALL TO ARMS: HOME

Sheffield and the English Civil War 1642–51

The Earl of Newark grew powerful in the North, he came with a strong army & besieged Rotherham. The Lieutenant was then at Chesterfield, only with 2 foot companies & 2 small [pieces] of ordnance, & being earnestly importuned by Sheffield men, & others to join with them & some promised forces from the Lord Fairfax, he went with a purpose to have joined with them & endeavour the raising of a siege. But as he was upon his march, a couple of our own solders that had been in Rotherham, during the siege, & found means to escape, by taking up arms for ye enemy, came & told him the Town was taken, Sheffield Castle quit, most of the honest men fled & not any hope of help from the Lord Fairfax, the Lieutenant Colonel, with those 2 companies & ordnance returned to Derby which the enemy might easily have cut off if he had certainly known in what condition we were.

Modernized text taken from Sir John Gell's account of events in the Midlands,
October 1642 to February 1643

The English Civil War that broke out in 1642 polarized large swathes of England into two distinctive camps: Parliamentarian and Royalist. Political tensions between Charles I and his parliament had been simmering for some time, as the cameral body grew increasingly dissatisfied with the monarch's absolute exercise of his authority.

The situation in the Midlands was particularly fluid as the fortunes of the opposing antagonists oscillated in a seemingly perpetual cycle. Towns with castles carried promise of strategic value, thus becoming the sites of armed siege and conflict. Sheffield was one such town where occupation between the Royalists and Parliamentarians fluctuated. The pivotal action was the ten-day Parliamentarian siege of Sheffield in August 1644.

Charles I.

Whereas it hath pleased almightie God to call to his mercy our Late soveraign Lord King James of happie memorie, By whose decease the Imperyall Crownes of Great Bryttaine, Fraunce & Ireland are rightfully to the high & Illustrious Prince Charles, Prince of Wales, Duke of Cornwall, Earle of Chester.

Wee therefore here now assembled, Doe hereby with one voice publishe & proclaime that the high & mightie Prince Charles is now by the Death of our Late Soveraign Lord King James of blessed memorie, Become our onely Lawfull, Lineall, & rightfull king, (Charles by the grace of God, King of greate Brittaine, Fraunce, & Ireland, Defendor of the fayth) To whome wee doe acknowledg al fayth and constant obedience with al hartie & humble Affection.

God save King Charles

Ashbie DeLazouche the 2nd of Aprill 1625

The landlord of Sheffield Manor at this time was staunch Royalist Thomas Howard, the 21st Earl of Arundel and 1st Earl of Norfolk. By choice, however, Howard did not reside on his estates, and when hostilities erupted in the Midlands he fled to the relative safety of the continent. In June 1642, Howard endorsed his loyalty to the Crown by having artillery pieces moved from Sheffield to Doncaster and placed at the disposal of Royalist forces in the town.

By 1640, and at a time in its history when Sheffield was rapidly gaining prominence as a manufacturing centre of steel products, the town had become largely pro-Parliamentarian. Leading figures and respected families in the community publicly announced their allegiance to Parliament's cause. The leading Parliamentarian activist in Sheffield was Sir John Bright of Carbook, who enlisted with Sir Thomas Fairfax's forces where he eventually was given the rank of colonel.

Refusing to accede to Parliament's demands for a devolution of power from the Crown, Charles I threw down the gauntlet when he raised his Royal standard at Nottingham Castle on 22 August 1642 – a symbolic declaration of war.

The Sheffield area prepared for war, with contemporary church records listing the acquisition of muskets, amour, swords, uniforms, and food and drink. William Cavendish, Earl of Newcastle, was appointed commander of Royalist forces in the northern counties, while Thomas Fairfax became the Parliamentarian counterpart.

In September 1642, in what is recognized as one of the first acts of war in Sheffield, 300 Northumberland cavaliers, commanded by Captain Grey, conducted an assault on the Great Houghton home of Parliamentarian Sir Edward Rhodes. A numerically superior force of Parliamentarians beat off the Royalists, sending them fleeing to Mansfield.

The following month, Parliamentarian commander Sir John Gell arrived at Sheffield and took control of the town and the strategically important castle. Towards the end of the year, Royalist Sir John Reresby attempted to smuggle four cannons out of Sheffield so that

Civil War re-enactment. (Photo Barry Skeates)

they would not fall into enemy hands. Trying such an act in a pro-Parliament town would prove the downfall of his plan, and the field pieces became part of Gell's armaments.

In 1643, the Earl of Newcastle led a Royalist army of 8,000 troops into the county of Yorkshire. He soon discovered that his presence was unwelcome in a region where Royalist supporters were very scarce. Only York stood out as an isolated island of Royalist loyalty. Newcastle, set on addressing the unsatisfactory status quo, started on a southbound crusade to establish the Crown's authority by force. Establishing garrisons in the name of the monarch at Tadcaster and Pontefract, Newcastle then evicted the Parliamentarians, including Fairfax father and son, from Leeds and Wakefield. Now firmly ensconced in the Parliamentarian heartland, Newcastle made Wakefield his operational headquarters, using the garrison as his springboard to launch an all-out attack on Rotherham and Sheffield. He knew that his hitherto uncompromising and highly successful display and employment of force, responsible for the string of military successes down the county, had to continue undiminished in intensity.

Newcastle took Rotherham and turned his attention to the much larger neighbouring town of Sheffield, where the town's castle presented the ultimate prize for his unstoppable army. After resting up for a few days, he marched on Sheffield. The town, however, fell unopposed. Hearing of the Royalist's string of successes in the county, the Parliamentarian garrison had deserted Sheffield and fled to Derbyshire.

Newcastle immediately set about strengthening his position. After imposing his authority on an unsupportive populace, the earl contracted local foundries to cast cannon to bolster his defences, and to manufacture other armaments required for the increase in his forces through local recruitment. In May, Sir William Savile, former MP for Yorkshire and a Royalist at heart, was appointed as commander of Sheffield and its castle.

This then allowed the now self-assured Newcastle to look across the county boundary at Derbyshire, where Sir John Gell and the Parliamentarians held sway. Any designs he had to restore Derbyshire to the Crown, however, were negated when Fairfax attacked his headquarters at Wakefield.

Savile's tenure as commander-in-chief and governor of Sheffield was short-lived. Upon his transfer to the strategically important garrison at York, Deputy Governor Thomas Beaumont was appointed to take his place. Savile would be killed in action the following year when fighting for the monarch at York.

In the strife-ridden England of 1643, skirmishes and battles occurred between Royalist and Parliamentarian forces at flashpoints across the nation. At the Battle of Adwalton on 30 June 1643, the 10,000-strong army of the Earl of Newcastle defeated Sir Thomas Fairfax at a spot twenty-six miles north of Sheffield. Garrisoned in Bradford at the time, Fairfax knew that the town would not last long against a Royalist siege, so he went out to challenge the advancing Newcastle with a much smaller force of between 3,000 and 4,000 troops. Against such odds, the outcome was inevitable, and the Fairfaxes fled the battlefield for Hull. This gave the victorious Newcastle the means and the impetus to retake the West Riding and Wakefield garrisons. The Royalist hold on Yorkshire, however, was short-lived.

While the Parliamentarian-controlled waters of the Irish Sea significantly reduced the flow of Irish recruits into the English king's armies, the Palace of Westminster had entered into an alliance with the Scots. Titled 'The Solemn League and Covenant', and signed on 25 September 1643, the pact was the brainchild of leading Parliamentarian and anti-Royalist activist, John Pym.

Early in January 1644, a well-armed Scottish army in excess of 20,000 crossed the River Tweed onto English soil. With the objective of wresting control of the north from the Royalists, the Scottish commander, the Earl of Leven, drew Newcastle out to meet him, and in doing so, allowed the Fairfaxes to march on York. Completing the three-pronged encirclement of York, the Earl of Manchester marched his Parliamentary Eastern Association Army in from the south. Newcastle, now a marquis, retired into York.

Hearing of the beleaguered Royalist garrison, Royalist commander and nephew to the King, Prince Rupert of the Rhine, moved his forces across from Lancashire. At the same time, Newcastle marched six miles out of York to face his enemy on Marston Moor. On 2 July, the combined Scottish Covenanters and Parliamentarian forces, including Oliver Cromwell, inflicted a costly defeat of the Royalists. Out of a force of 17,500, 4,000 Royalist soldiers lost their lives on the battlefield and a further 1,500 were taken prisoner. The Parliamentarians lost 300 men. Parliament was now ready to retake Sheffield Castle.

On 27 July, the Earl of Manchester sent a message to the Royalist garrison instructing them to relinquish their hold on Sheffield. Days later, Manchester despatched a force of 1,200 men under Major General Crawford and Colonel Pickering to force Royalist compliance.

Sir Thomas Fairfax, Parliamentary general.

SIR THOMAS FAIRFAX *Knight.*
General of the Forces raised by the Parliament.

On 1 August, Crawford commenced his bombardment, but he was unable to breach the castle walls as his 4in. demi-culverin artillery pieces proved inadequate. Heavier calibre guns were requested from Fairfax, who was able supply the besiegers with 6in. demi-cannons and 5.5in. culverins.

While reconnoitring the castle walls on the 3rd in search of a potential weak spot in the stone walls, Captain Sands of the Parliamentarian Pioneers and the artillery master gunner were shot at from the castle ramparts. Both were fatally wounded. Two days later, after regular shelling of the castle, Crawford once more called on the Royalists to surrender. The governor, Thomas Beaumont, responded in no uncertain terms that the king had entrusted him to hold the castle and, valuing the monarch's commission more than his own life, refused to yield.

That night, Crawford tried to employ local miners to tunnel a way into the castle. The fact that the building sat on solid rock put paid to the general's latest attempt to end the siege in his favour.

On 10 August, the castle defenders eventually capitulated. The instruments of surrender required the Royalists to hand over all war matériel in return for unhindered passage for Governor Beaumont, and his officers and men to Pontefract Castle. Included in those allowed to leave Sheffield unhindered were all the soldiers' wives and children, including Lady Savile, her family and her entourage and personal goods. Heavily pregnant at the time of the siege, Lady Savile, widowed when her husband and erstwhile governor of Sheffield Castle was killed in battle at York in January 1644, went into labour the night after the castle fell to the Parliamentarians.

After appointing Colonel John Bright of Carbook Hall as governor of Sheffield Castle, Crawford marched on to Staveley Hall, Bolsover Castle and Wingfield to dislodge the Royalist garrisons.

At Sheffield, Bright was replaced as governor by Captain Edward Hill of Carr House in Rotherham, when the former took up the position of military governor of York. Cementing the Parliamentary hold on Sheffield, a body of commissioners confiscated estates around the town that belonged to Royalists such as the absent Thomas Howard, Lord of Sheffield Manor.

To ensure that Sheffield Castle – as well as others in the country – no longer lured Royalist forces for its strategic value, in April 1646, Whitehall determined that the fortress be rendered unfit for purpose. A year later, a more finite instruction from the House of Commons ordered the castle to be levelled to the ground. In August 1648, demolition work commenced.

In November, Thomas Howard's son, Henry Frederick, 22nd Earl of Arundel, paid a massive fine of £6,000 for the restitution of family estates at Sheffield, before repurchasing

Cromwell's soldiers break into a Royalist house. (Work by J. Williamson)

> This prynce [Rupert] after a long seige & with loss of many men tooke ye close at Leichfeild, but instead of coming on to Derby he returned back to Oxford, but left a Garison at
>
> Burton with ye Lord Grey & wee tooke presently after and there wee placed Captaine Sanders with his Company.
>
> Whilst these things were in ... ye Earle of Newarke grewe powerfull in ye North, he came with a strong armie & beseiged Rotheram. Ye Liefetennant was then at Chesterfeild, onely with 2 foote companies & 2 small ... of ordynance, & being ernestly importuned by Sheaffeild men, & others to joyne with them & some promised forces from ye Lord Fayrfax, he went with a purpose to have joyned with them & endevour ye raiseing of a seige. But as he was upon his marche, a couple of our owne souldyers yt had been in Rotheram, during ye seige, & found meanes to escape, by takeing up armes for ye enemie, came & told hym ye Towne was taken, Sheaffeild Castle quitt, most of ye honest men fledd & not any hope of help from ye Lord Fayrfax, the Liefetennant Collonell, with those 2 companies & ordynance returned to Derby wich y enemie might easely have cutt off if he had certenly knowne in what condition we were.
>
> A true account of y raising & imployering of one foote Regiment under Sr. John Gell from y beginning of October 1642 until y midle of February 1643

the castle in 1649. By this time, however, demolition work was at such an advanced state, that it could not be saved. It would no longer be a prize in military conflict.

Mutiny in Sheffield, 1795

Britain's war with France since 1793 had placed enormous pressure of wheat supplies as large volumes of the local crop was bought up to feed the warring army and navy. The war in itself hindered the import of wheat to alleviate the shortages at home.

The unseasonal hot, dry summer of 1794 resulted in a very poor wheat crop, further aggravating the situation and pushing the nation to the brink of widespread starvation. A bitterly cold winter followed. The lot of the poor and the working class quickly proved fertile ground for civil unrest, ultimately leading to the so-called Bread Riots the following year.

In early August 1795, however, the mischievous distribution of 'inflammatory handbills' as a result of bread shortages fomented levels of dissent which spilled into the ranks of the military. Incidents of disobedience and mutiny ensued.

Copy of the Hand Bill referred to above.
Treason! Treason! Treason!
Against the People!
The People's humbugg'd! a plot is discovered!

Pitt and the Committee for Bread are combined
Together to starve the Poor into the Army and Navy!
And to starve your Widows and Orphans!
God held ye Labourers of the Nation!
You are held in requisition to fight in a bad cause;
A cause that is blasted by Heaven! And damned by all good men!
Every man to his tent, O! Israel;
Sharpen your weapons, and spare not! For all
The Scrats in the nation are united against your
Blood, your wives, and your little ones!
Behold good Bread at Six Shillings per Stone;
And may every wearer of a Bayonet be struck with
Heaven's loudest Thunder, that refuses to help you!
Fear not your lives! Aristocrats are scoundrels,
Cowards. Cursed be the framers and promoters
Of the Corn Bill! And let all the People say
Amen!

On the 4th, a corn dealer's wheat being transported by wagon through Pontefract was hijacked:

At nine in the evening two of his [corn dealer] waggons, laden with corn, had entered town, on their way to the west; the alarm spread like wildfire, and in less than ten minutes there were women in the market place, armed with knives, who immediately seized the waggons and horses, ripped every sack, and spread the corn about the streets.

Kentish Gazette, Friday, 14 August 1795

As the situation worsened, local authorities started resorting to calling out the military to address the volatile situation. In Bishopsford, the magistrate read the Riot Act and called out the Fencible Cavalry. In one town in Essex, the civil power found that the deployment of a platoon of the Surrey Fencible Cavalry had no impact on the rioters. Soldiers were pulled off their horses and attacked with pitchforks. Reinforcements in the form of grenadier and light infantry companies of the Wiltshire Militia were summoned. In Suffolk, a detachment of the Ipswich-based Norfolk Cavalry had to go in to quell unrest. In Peterborough, it was the Volunteer Yeomanry that had to be called out, in Cambridgeshire, the local yeomanry.

In Exeter, Lord Conyngham marched his Londonderry Regiment on to the city's parade ground where they were to be absorbed by the 43rd Regiment of Foot. The men of the Londonderry were unhappy with the merger, openly expressing their dissatisfaction and refusing to obey orders from the 43rd's commander, Colonel Dennison. The officers on parade drew their swords and warned the rebels that they all faced serious punishment. On being rude to Dennison, the colonel struck a private with his sword. At that, the two regiments were separated from each other while troops from the 25th Dragoons galloped onto the square to disarm the dissenters.

On Tuesday, 4 August, mutiny broke out in Sheffield.

Rumours had earlier reached the ears of the adjutant of the Loyal Independent Sheffield Volunteers that a combined mob of civilians and recruits from Colonel Cameron's Regiment was going to demonstrate against pay arrears comprising what was called 'bread money'. The adjutant called out the Volunteers' officers who decided to 'put the Volunteers under arms'. A message would immediately be sent to the regiment's commanding officer, Colonel R. A. Athorpe, who was away from Sheffield at the time.

At 6 pm that evening, Cameron conducted the usual parade of the recruits, watched on this occasion by some 300 'spectators'. The crowd quickly swelled to 'several thousands', resulting in Cameron making a decision to dismiss the recruits and order them back to their barracks. At this, however, elements of the crowd shouted at the recruits to ignore the order to dismiss and to remain where they were. Undaunted, Cameron stood his ground and re-issued his command for the recruits to dismiss. This precipitated increased belligerence from the rabble, with calls of 'damn him – stab him – kill him – stick him – and [that] made use of other such expressions'.

Contemporary satire of how the wealthy coped with chronic wheat shortages that led to the Bread Riots of 1795.

Immediately acting on this dangerous turn of events, the Sheffield Volunteers' adjutant, who also held the same position in Cameron's regiment, went to rally the Volunteers. He ranked his men in Norfolk Street adjoining the parade ground, where the Colonel Athorpe joined them.

Athorpe addressed the agitated crowd directly, exhorting them to disperse and go home in a peaceful manner. Athorpe's request was ignored, the mob complaining about the bread shortage. Athorpe continued to remonstrate with them, stating that he would do everything in his power to address and resolve their issues.

With the commission to do so, Athorpe read out the Riot Act. Ninety minutes later, and the mob had spread out onto the street and into surrounding yards and crofts. At this point, missiles started being thrown at the Volunteers. Several soldiers were struck, including one who suffered a deep gash when a piece of brick struck him on the cheek. Athorpe now accepted that immediate decisive steps had to be taken to prevent his men from being overwhelmed. He ordered the front rank to open fire directly at the mob from a distance of 50 yards. Two were killed and the mob fled in all directions.

As investigations commenced afterwards, it was discovered that many of the recruits had come on parade with stones in their pockets, a clear indication that there was going to be trouble. Other recruits had gone to a local merchant to acquire scythes and pitchforks, but had been unsuccessful as the owner refused to part with any.

That night and the next day, the Oxford Blues and the West Riding Cavalry from Rotherham were deployed into Sheffield. They were armed and were distributing leaflets produced by the magistrates telling everyone to stay at home, and 'masters of families to prevent their servants and apprentices going into the streets'.

A letter from a 'gentleman' belonging to the Sheffield Independent Volunteers appeared in the 8 August *Hull Advertiser and Exchange Gazette*:

> This place has been a scene of confusion for these two days past, owing to a company of soldiers which are now raising here, having mutinied against their officers. We have been under arms for thirty-six hours, having been obliged to fire upon the mob, and am sorry to say have killed two men. We are however now quiet and peaceable.

The 6-pdr Town Guns were made for the Sheffield Loyal Independent Volunteers, as a precaution against any possible internal revolt and foreign invasion. The guns, widely used by British artillery, had barrels that were 5 feet long. They had a range of 350 yards with the barrel level, and a range of 2,000 yards if the barrel was elevated by 10 per cent.

Local folklore has it that the town guns were fired on the day of the riots, but there is no evidence to support this.

Luddite Riots: Sheffield Local Militia, 1812

Towards the end of 1811, civil unrest erupted in Nottinghamshire caused by widespread resistance to the proposed mechanization of the wool and cotton weaving industry. Up to this point weaving had largely been driven by cottage-industry-type commercial activity, in which production relied on stocking-frame knitters in private homes. Mechanical looms would pose a direct threat to jobs and income at this traditional level.

It is generally believed that the name Luddite was derived from a young stocking-frame knitter, Nedd Ludd, who demolished two weaving frames in anger in 1770. The etymology of the name was then absorbed into folklore when many ardently held that the movement's name came from a mythical persona who lived in the Sherwood Forest, by the name of General or King Ned Ludd.

By November, the scale of the unrest had grown to a level of violence that precipitated the mobilization of troops to restore the rule of law. Uncontrolled mobs targeted stocking-frame owners and wrecked their machines. As the magnitude of the unruly behaviour grew, mill operators, including corn millers, were also targeted. The deployment of local militia and two troops of light dragoons turned Nottingham into a garrison.

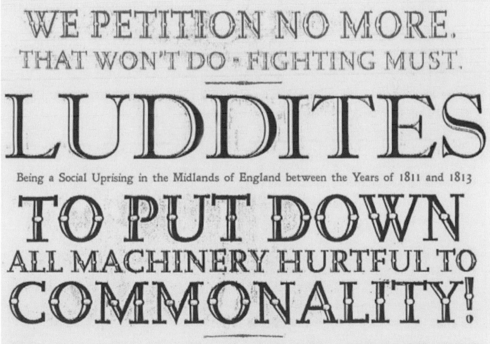

"Certain inventions in machinery were introduced into the staple manufacturers of the north, which, greatly reducing the numbers of hands necessary to be employed, threw thousands out of work, and left them without legitimate means of sustaining life..."

WE PETITION NO MORE,
THAT WON'T DO - FIGHTING MUST.

LUDDITES

Being a Social Uprising in the Midlands of England between the Years of 1811 and 1813

TO PUT DOWN
ALL MACHINERY HURTFUL TO
COMMONALITY!

"Misery generates hate; these sufferers hated the machines which they believed took their bread from them; they hated the buildings which contained those machines; they hated the manufacturers who owned those buildings." -Charlotte Brontë, *Shirley*

Luddite propaganda.

By February 1812, the riots had spread into neighbouring counties, including Lancashire and Yorkshire, resulting in the further deployment of troops from as far afield as Somerset, West Essex, Edinburgh and Surrey.

Huddersfield was particularly badly hit by the savagery of the wanton destruction of weaving mills. Face-blackened rioters completely demolished frames, shears and ancillary equipment at Big Mills, Marsh. The *Leeds Mercury* of 29 February, described the modus operandi of the Luddites in that part of Yorkshire:

The depredators, or to use the cant terms, Luddites, assemble with as much privacy as possible, at the place marked out for attack, and divide themselves into two parties, the more daring and expert of which enter the premises, provided with proper implements for the work of destruction, which they accomplish with astonishing secrecy and despatch. The other part remains conveniently stationed at the outside of the building, to keep off all intruders, or to give the alarm, if a superior force, was likely to be opposed to them.

As soon as the work of destruction was completed, the Leader drew up his men, called over the roll, each man answering to a particular number instead of his name; they then fired off their pistols, (for they were armed), gave a shout, and marched off in regular military order.

THE LUDDITES

With infinite presumption they [Luddites] have attributed the gradual pacification of the disturbed districts to their exertions in storming Government to relinquish its retaliatory measures; but the fact is, that the state of work and wages remains nearly the same as before the alteration in the Orders in Council, while the price of provisions is much advanced. The quantity of distress is, unhappily, undiminished, and yet the Luddite system is breaking up.

The Luddites have felt themselves insecure; on every side the law drew its circle round them; and this insecurity has obliged many of them to abscond, or to secrete themselves.

In this state of uncertainty and alarm, the clemency of Government has had an effectual operation; we hope, too, a lasting one, for they will have learned much in vain it is to contend with such a state of society, held together by so many bonds, and guaranteed by so mighty a power, as that which exists in Great Britain.

But let the men in higher stations, whose political violence has misled and prevented the lower class, blush for the mischievous effects of their speeches, writings, and example. To them, in truth, much of the mischief that has been perpetrated, is to be attributed.

London Courier and Evening Gazette, Friday, 4 September 1812

They do not appear to have done any mischief besides breaking the machinery; and one of the party having asked the Leader what they should do with one of the Proprietors, he replied, hurt not a hair of his head; but that should they be under the necessity of visiting him again, they should not shew him any mercy.

Concerned magistrates in Huddersfield sought assistance from General Vyse at Beverley, who responded immediately by ordering a troop of 'Scotch Grey's' to night-march to Huddersfield. With the situation volatile in the county, a squadron of cavalry was despatched from Sheffield to Beverley to fill the void left by the Scottish troops. Upon the arrival in Huddersfield two days later of a squadron of the 2nd Dragoon Guards from York, the Scotch Guards returned to Beverley and, in turn, Sheffield's cavalry.

In the afternoon of 14 April, in a shocking development in the pernicious unrest, and with undertones of revolution, the armoury at the Sheffield Local Militia depot was stormed and broken into.

At the Yorkshire Summer Assizes in York on Thursday 21 July, Joseph Wolstenholme (17), John Rowan (15), William Rodgers (16) and Mary Gibbons (48), were charged with 'a misdemeanour, in riotously assembling, and breaking into the depot of the Local Militia, at Sheffield'.

Sergeant Thomas Flathes of the Sheffield Local Militia, lived near the depot and was on duty when the mob arrived at the depot. He informed the jury how he had seen 'about five or six men and about forty or fifty boys' coming towards the depot, which was situated a short distance from the town. When they arrived at the turnpike about thirty yards from the depot, they halted and were joined by 'an immense mob, four or five thousand persons'.

After a short while, several of the rioters pointed at 'arms in the depot', which appear to have been visible through the windows. A massive barrage of stones ensued, in which the windows were 'almost instantly demolished'. The mob then swarmed into the depot courtyard, determined to get to the arms inside. Dislodging a large stone from a wall, a few of the rioters forced the door open. As one of them started to enter, Sergeant Flathes, who had been inside with Captain Best, confronted him, wielding a 'musket with his bayonet fixed'. Flathes threatened to run him through, but having retreated momentarily, the mob started stoning the lone soldier. Flathes then ducked into his adjoining house to protect his wife and three young children. From an upstairs window, he watched helplessly as the rioters, surprisingly, revealed that they were there not to pilfer, but to destroy. He told the court that he had observed one man smashing a dozen muskets against a wall.

About twenty minutes later, a party of dragoons arrived, causing the rioters to flee. Out of the armoury of 900 muskets, 300 were destroyed. Flathes pointed out to the court that one of the accused, Mary Gibbons, was seen to drop a parcel as she fled before the dragoons. The parcel was found to contain 'two pair of military pantaloons and a pair of gaiters'.

The prosecutor, who protested that the charges against them had been too lenient in the first instance, despaired as two of the four accused were acquitted.

On 18 April, a regimental court martial, convened in Huddersfield to hear a charge against a private accused of misconduct, sentenced the soldier to 300 lashes, a shocking

'Leader of the Luddites'.

indictment of military law of the day. The unfortunate soldier had been found guilty of neglect of duty by 'refusing or neglecting to defend it [Rawfolds Mill] in the manner he ought to have done'. The following morning, he was escorted by a party of dragoons to the mill, so that the owner, a Mr Cartwright, could be witness to the private receiving his punishment. After about twenty-five lashes, however, Cartwright had seen enough and interceded on behalf of the soldier. The remainder of the punishment was 'remitted'.

In January 1813, the special commission convened at York announced their determination of sixty-six individuals charged with Luddite riots. Seventeen would be executed, six transported for seven years, seven acquitted, seventeen discharged on bail, fifteen discharged by proclamation, and one indicted for future assizes.

In May, a disturbing report was received about the deteriorating situation at Huddersfield, thirty miles north of Sheffield:

I am sorry to inform you the Luddites have been very active in collecting arms this last week, and have been too successful. They proceeded to people's houses, in the townships of Almondbury, Wooldale, Farnley, Netherthong, Meltham, Honley and Marsden, and many other places in this neighbourhood; they entered the houses by about 20 or 30 in a gang, and demanded all the arms in the house, on pain of instant death. By this means they have obtained possession of upwards of 100 stand of arms since my last letter to you, and not one night has passed without some arms having so been taken.

In order to check this alarming evil, Major Gordon has obtained possession of 200 stand of arms from the inhabitants of this neighbourhood; the military are in this manner daily employed in collecting arms, but they have not yet been fortunate enough to discover the depot of the Luddites.

Leeds Mercury, Saturday, 9 May 1812

3. CALL TO ARMS: FOREIGN

The Alexandra Redoubt, New Zealand, 1863

Arising out of the British colonization of New Zealand, which had to led to widespread Maori resistance on the North Island, the Treaty of Waitingi was signed on 6 February 1840. Tensions continued to simmer, however, and on two occasions this erupted into fighting between the two parties: 1845–47 and 1863–65.

For the British, Tuakau was a useful revictualling stopover for troops travelling between Auckland and the Waikato. Until 1863, relations between the Maoris and the itinerant troops of the empire were largely cordial. In that year, troubles started to occur, leading the British to place a temporary force in the area.

In July 1863, 300 troops of the 65th (2nd Yorkshire, North Riding) Regiment of Foot were despatched from Drury to establish a garrison at Tuakau. Selecting a high knoll with a commanding view over the westward-flowing Waikato River, the detachment set about constructing a fortification which was named the Alexandra Redoubt, in honour of the Princess of Wales. Sporting the sobriquet 'Royal Tigers', the warrior-like Maori in the district, due to their inability to say '65th', referred to the regiment as the 'Hickety Pip'.

Strategically, the British stronghold was put in place to protect the planned invasion of Waikato as the advance moved up the river from the sea, safeguarding Lieutenant General D. A. Cameron's right flank.

The 65th Regiment parade in full dress uniform, Mt Eliot, New Plymouth, New Zealand, March 1861. (Photo Bruce Cairns)

A MATCH FOR THE MAORIES

The Auckland correspondent of the *New Zealand Examiner* writes:

To give you an idea of his [New Zealand Governor Sir George Grey] tact and skill in seizing hold of every opening afforded by his opponents, I may relate the clever manoeuvre under cover of which he carried his predetermined point of moving a large number of troops on to the frontiers of Waikato.

When he visited [the Kingites in] Waikato, the leading men of the King party had arranged that a guard of honour, consisting of twenty men from each of the tribes adhering to the King movement, should alternately attend upon Matutaura, and by their presence convince the Governor that the Maori King was, in their estimation at least of his own people, equal in dignity to the representative of the Queen. Sir George was well aware of this.

[Sir George:] 'I hear you have appointed a guard of twenty men to take care of your King.' 'Oh, yes,' was the reply, 'have we not the right to do so?'

'Well, perhaps it may be all right,' replied Sir George, 'at all events I shan't attempt to prevent you. But if you consider your own man in such danger as to require twenty men, armed, to be constantly with him to protect him, I shall require a great number of men to take care of all my "pakehas" [non-Maoris], who are scattered up and down the country, and I shall at once send 2,000 soldiers to Mugatawhiri.'

The chiefs were nonplussed at this piece of effrontery, and at first treated it as a joke.

'Kahore [no],' said they, 'you are only humbugging us. What do you want with soldiers so near Waikato? We shan't hurt your pakehas, but we don't like your soldiers to come here.'

'Oh, no. I'm not joking,' was the quick rejoinder, 'it is only fair that, if your one man requires a guard of twenty soldiers, my hundreds of men, belonging to the Queen, require a guard too; and a guard of 2,000 men they shall have, whether you like it or not.'

According to Maori idea this logic was unanswerable, as the discomfited chiefs were compelled to grin and bear it.

Fife Herald, Thursday, 10 April 1862

It only took two weeks for the 65th to complete the construction of the redoubt, which basically amounted to deep defensive ditches, corner bastions and stepped parapets. Some 360 roughly hewn steps led down to the river, the only source of water for the garrison. At this point, the redoubt strength was reduced by half and Captain Richard Swift appointed officer commanding of the garrison.

Whilst the redoubt never faced a direct assault, an engagement with the local tribe by elements of the 65th from the redoubt, has been lauded as one of the most remarkable of the so-called New Zealand Wars.

Provisions arriving by ship at Port Waikato were transported by friendly Maoris to a British supply depot, Cameron Town, seven miles downriver from Tuakau. Three white men were stationed at Cameron Town, including Resident Magistrate Armitage to administer the flow of supplies. The other two Europeans were known only as Robert and William.

On 7 September 1863, 200 Kingite warriors from South Waikato launched a surprise attack on Camerontown, murdering the three Englishmen there. Robert and William were both shot and fell into the river; their bodies were never recovered. Captain Swift responded immediately, setting off for the depot with his lieutenant, three sergeants, a drummer and fifty troops.

Upon reaching the bush around Cameron Town after a three-hour march, voices were heard in the scrub and Swift ordered the attack. They had been expected, however, and walked into an ambush. Swift immediately took a hit as the concealed Maoris opened fire. He succumbed to his wound later that night. Fellow officer and second-in-command, Lieutenant Butler also went down. The senior NCO, Colour Sergeant Edward McKenna then assumed command, and courageously led a charge against the Maori line, but the

enemy's numbers were too great. McKenna then took the decision to sit tight until dark to retire. Espying warriors manoeuvring around their rear to cut off their escape route, McKenna rallied the troops and charged the enemy a second time. Their effort to take the enemy line was met with a hail of bullets, leaving one dead and three wounded.

As the light began to fade, McKenna took his men down from the hill where they had encountered the Maoris, to an area of thick bush to wait the night out. At first light, McKenna led the men back towards the redoubt. En route, they were met by a relief party from the redoubt and returned safely to the garrison.

In a 22 December 1863-gazetted despatch from Commanding Officer of the 65th, Lieutenant Colonel Alfred Wyatt, McKenna's report on the engagement was included. After 'proceeding in

Colour Sergeant Samuel Scammell, 65th Regiment, died of dysentery at New Plymouth, New Zealand on 18 April 1861. (Photo Bruce Cairns)

skirmishing order', the detachment paused on a path on which the *pā* – Maori settlement – was situated. Here Captain Swift ordered the distribution of a 'half ration of rum'
before continuing towards the supply depot. McKenna continues:

After advancing in this order for about three-quarters of a mile, I observed tracks of
natives, and in large numbers. This I pointed out to the Captain, and a little further on,
I heard the natives in loud debate, on which (expecting that they were returning on the
track that we were pursuing) I again informed Captain Swift, who ordered the men to
lie down in the bush, at the same time ordering them not to fire until he gave the word
of command.

However, on finding that the natives were not advancing, I crept up to within twelve
yards of them, when, from their conversation, I judged that they were under the influence
of liquor. Captain Swift immediately called to advance, ordering the men to fix bayonets
and charge. We advanced to within six yards of them, when they opened a most terrific
fire. Captain Swift and Lieutenant Butler were at this time leading on the men, and after
receiving the enemy's fire, the men gave a cheer and returned it in grand style. Lieutenant
Butler shooting down a native on his right, turned his revolver to the left. As quick as a
thought I saw him come on his knee, at the same time discharging the remainder of the
barrels of his revolver, bringing another native down at the same time that he fell himself.

Seeing that he was wounded, I ordered Lance-Corporal Ryan and one of the men to
take him to the rear, when he ordered me to lead the men to the front. On turning to my
left, I found Captain Swift mortally wounded, and after speaking a few words to him he
desired me to take his revolver and lead on the men, as that time I was loading. With
one loud huzza we charged like demons, burning to revenge our officers. I now found
myself in an open clearing of a few yards, the rebels flying to cover on our front and left,
where they opened fire on my small party, who at this time numbered two Serjeants, one
bugler, and thirty-five men.

Seeing that we were greatly outnumbered, I determined to hold our position, if
possible, until dark, trusting that the men in charge of Captain Swift and Lieutenant
Butler had retired well to the rear, and been joined with our lost advanced guard; if
so, I knew they would be able to make well towards the redoubt – before darkness set
in, when, probably, I should be able to join them, but I found at about a quarter to six
o'clock that the enemy had got round to our rear, thereby cutting off our retreat by the
way we came. I immediately ordered a charge, but was met by a volley that killed one
and wounded three men. On trying again, I found it hopeless to attempt it, I therefore
determined to retreat down the hill, which was covered with fern, and, sending on our
wounded, I threw out a line of skirmishers, ordering the front rank to 'fire and retire.' In
this order we retired down the hill in a steady and orderly manner, the natives coming
out of the bush and raining down a complete shower of bullets on us, when, although we
were not above 100 or 150 yards from them, not a man was hit.

At this time it was near dark, but we managed to scramble through the bush until at
last we lost the track, when I ordered the men around me, and told them I should stay

there until morning, ordering not a word to be spoken, or a pipe to be lighted. I now found that four of the men were missing, and knowing that it would be completely useless to attempt at that time to find them, I determined to wait until morning, hoping in the meantime to hear them about in the bush. At a quarter to five o'clock, A.M., on the morning of the 8th, we commenced to try and gain a track out of the bush, and at about eight o'clock, A.M., we succeeded, and were met about half-way from the redoubt by Colonel Murray and his party, and then learned that our esteemed Captain was dead.

After detailing a man to return as guide to Colonel Murray, I continued my march to the camp, which we reached at about eleven o'clock, A.M., completely exhausted. I am very sorry to report our casualties were very great; but, taking into consideration the number to which we were opposed, being near seven to one, we have every reason to be thankful that it was not greater. I hope it may not appear presumptuous on my part to bear testimony to the cool and gallant manner displayed by the late Captain Swift and Lieutenant Butler in this desperate affair, the Captain issuing his commands as if on parade, and even, when wounded, refusing to take one man from the force to take him to the rear until he was told that I would not be able to keep my position much longer; and Lieutenant Butler, even when brought on his knees, in the coolest manner possible, deliberately fired the shots from his revolver into a crowd of Maories. I need scarcely add that

Light company NCOs and men, 65th Regiment, New Zealand. (Photo Bruce Cairns)

the men behaved most gallantly, in fact it would be impossible to recapitulate the many acts of individual courage, when each man emulated the other in acts of heroic bravery.

I, however, beg to bring to your favourable consideration the valuable assistance I received from Serjeant Bracegirdle, who supported me throughout in a most intrepid manner, as also Lance-Corporal Ryan, Privates William Bulford, John Talbot, John Pole, and Benjamin Thomas, for the devotion they manifested to their officers, by staying with them until half-past seven P.M. on the night of the 7th instant. Captain Swift died at that time, after which they hid his body in the bush and waited until morning, and then carrying the Lieutenant in their arms they returned, meeting Colonel Murray and force. Lance Corporal Ryan returned with Colonel Murray, and pointed out the spot in which Captain Swift's body was.

I should estimate the loss of the enemy to be between twenty and thirty in killed and wounded, seven of whom I, myself, distinctly saw shot dead and dragged into the bush by the rebels.

I remain, &c.

(Signed) E. McKENNA, Colour-Serjeant,

65th Regiment.

Casualties, when considering the circumstances, were relatively light. Captain Richard Swift (32) and privates Stephen Grace (37), Robert Bellinger (28) lost their lives. Private

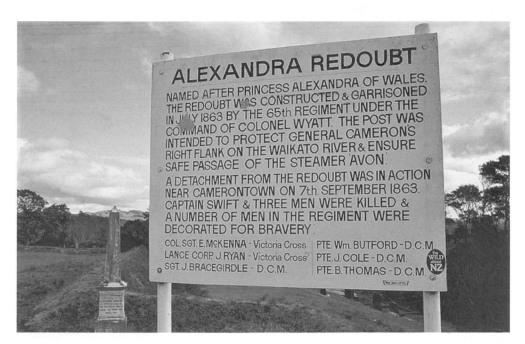

Alexandra Redoubt Memorial, Waikato, New Zealand, showing fortifications and cemetery. (Photo Brian Griffiths)

Michael Bryant (30) was initially reported as wounded and missing. What makes this small engagement in a little-known colonial war stand out in the annals of the history of the British army, however, is the number of bravery awards – eight – earned by those few men of the 65th.

Colour Sergeant Edward McKenna and Lance Corporal John Ryan were both awarded the Victoria Cross. McKenna was also given a commission. Tragically, Ryan drowned while trying to rescue a comrade on 29 December 1863. His Victoria Cross was therefore awarded posthumously.

Sergeants John Bracegirdle and Michael Meara, and privates William Bulford, John Cole, John Talbot and Benjamin Thomas were all awarded the Distinguished Conduct Medal.

Spioenkop, Anglo-Boer War, January 1900

Monday, 22 January

Paraded under arms about 4 am. Our Brigade was on Convoy Guard. After breakfast we had a bath in the Tugela. Had to lay about in the blazing sun all day. Felt properly done up. Fighting was going on in front of us which we could see plainly.

In the afternoon we were ordered to go to the front. We were not so long before we were in the firing line. When it came on dark, we were moving about the best part of the night getting into position for the morning. It was a terrible march up the hills. Every now and then one would fall over a boulder or else into a hollow. Then it commenced raining we got wet through.

At daybreak we were in the firing line, firing away as hard as we could go. We had our Maxim gun with us. We remained in the firing line till about 2 pm when we were relieved by the Border Regt. The enemy's bullets and shells were pouring around us like rain. We relieved the Border Regt. Again about 6 pm and held the position till about 8 am the following morning ... making about 49 hours in position and under fire. The average number of rounds fired by each man of the Regiment was about 500 and our rifles were like bars of hot iron.

Private W. A. Pye, West Yorkshire Regiment

On 12 December 1899, 24 officers and 838 other ranks of the 1st Battalion, the York and Lancaster Regiment (1/Yorks), embarked at Liverpool on board SS *Majestic* for deployment to the South African theatre of war. On 2 January 1900, the battalion disembarked at Durban in the British colony of Natal, from where they were sent to the British camp at Springfield on the northern outskirts of Durban. Here they formed part of Colonel J. F. Burn-Murdoch's 1st Cavalry Brigade, which also included the 1st Royal Dragoons, 13th and 14th Hussars, A Battery, Royal Horse Artillery (RHA), two naval 12-pounders and the Imperial Light Infantry.

From 2 November 1899, South African republican forces – usually referred to as Boers – numbering 21,000 men, laid siege to Ladysmith in Natal, trapping inside the British garrison, which had a strength of 572 officers and 12,924 other ranks, commanded by General Sir George White.

British artillery crossing a pontoon bridge over the Tugela River, Natal, Anglo-Boer War. (Photo Joanna Neal)

NATAL THREATENED

ALLEGED SERIOUS NEGLECT OF THE WAR OFFICE

A special correspondent of the *Morning Post*, reporting on a tour through Natal, says:

The town of Newcastle is utterly unprotected. It is within 14 miles of the Orange Free State border and eight miles of that of the Transvaal. If Newcastle is seized, the possession of Lang's [Laing's] Nek by the Boers is assured. The holding of Lang's Nek by the Boers will mean 20 miles of fighting over rough country, peculiarly suited to Boer tactics, before the British can begin the first real action.

Armed Boers frequently ride into Newcastle, and the local magistrate is utterly powerless, for he has only six policemen at his disposal. The nearest troops consist of a small detachment of Hussars posted on Sunday river watching De Beer's Pass.

The War Office needs waking up. The Boers of the Klip river district declare that they will invade Natal as soon as rain has fallen for two days. A commando of Utrecht burghers is already engaged in patrolling the Buffalo river. [The war started on 11 October 1899]

South Wales Daily News, Thursday, 7 September 1899

Commander of the British garrison, Sir George White's house, Ladysmith siege, Anglo-Boer War. (Photo Joanna Neal)

General Sir Redvers Buller VC, KCB, KCMG, at the time commanding officer at Aldershot, was selected as the 'best officer' to command British forces in South Africa. The reluctant Buller arrived in Cape Town at the end of October, where, upon assessing the situation, decided that the imperative was to relieve the besieged towns of Ladysmith and Kimberley before marching on Bloemfontein, the capital of the Orange Free State Republic. Assigning Lord Methuen to Kimberley, Buller at first allocated the relief of Ladysmith to Major General Francis Clery with two brigades, but he was then persuaded by his generals to personally head the campaign to relieve Ladysmith.

Assembling his force at Frere, about thirty miles south of Ladysmith, Buller faced a daunting task, strongly influenced by largely unmapped terrain. At Colenso ten miles to his north, was the large, meandering Tugela River, which could only be crossed by bridge, or where the Boers had blown up a bridge, by Royal Engineer pontoon. Here, Buller was faced with a formidable range of towering hills, rising to 1,500ft above the Tugela and running twenty-five miles along a west–east axis. From his far left, forming an amphitheatre overlooking Colenso, were Tabanyama, or Rangeworthy Heights, at 4,570ft, the steep-sided and tallest Spioenkop, Brakfontein and Vaalkrantz ridges, and, to the east of the road to Ladysmith, Tugela Heights and Hlangwhane Mountain.

In mid-December, Buller suffered the first major setback of his campaign to liberate Ladysmith. Major General Sir Fitzroy Hart misjudged the path of the Tugela as he sought to cross the river, resulting in 600 casualties being inflicted on his 5th (Irish) Brigade by General Louis Botha's forces. This was followed by the disastrous loss of ten of Colonel

The Colenso railway bridge over the Tugela River, blown up by republican forces, Anglo-Boer War. (Photo Joanna Neal)

Charles Long's field guns when two of his Royal Horse Artillery batteries came under deadly Boer fire in an exposed position. After what history would record as the Battle of Colenso, Buller retreated to Chievely to lick his wounds. Coming as the third major defeat in what became known in London as Black Week, the War Office immediately took the decision to send Lord Frederick Roberts VC to South Africa as Commander-in-Chief, instead of the disgraced Buller.

At this time, Buller's force was bolstered to 30,000 by the arrival in Estcourt on 8 January 1900 of the 5th Division under Lieutenant General Sir Charles Warren RE. Coming out of retirement after an unsuccessful period as commissioner of the Metropolitan Police (during the time of the Jack the Ripper murders), Warren led two infantry brigades, the 11th commanded by Major General Sir Edward Woodgate, and the 10th, under Major General John Talbot Coke. The four battalions making up the 11th Infantry Brigade were the 2nd Battalion, the King's Own Royal Lancasters (2/KORL), the 2nd Battalion, the Lancashire Fusiliers (2/Lancs), the 1st Battalion, the South Lancashire Regiment (1/S. Lancs), and the 1st Battalion the York and Lancaster Regiment (1/Yorks).

In his second attempt to force his way through the Boer front to reach Ladysmith, on 10 January, Buller set off to the west with a column of 23,000 troops and 650 support ox wagons – a lumbering seventeen miles long. In a four-mile-wide basin of great loops in the Tugela, Buller spilt the force in two. Major General Neville Lyttleton would take one half of the force and cross the Tugela at Potgieter's Drift, while Warren would cross at Trichardt's Drift a further five miles upstream.

On 15 January, Buller issued 'secret' orders to Warren, who was now camped on Mount Alice, just to the south of Potgieter's Drift.

1. The enemy's position in front of Potgieter's Drift seems to me to be too strong to be taken by direct attack.
2. I intend to try and turn it by sending a force across the Tugela from near Trickhardt's [sic] Drift and up to the west of Spion Kop.
3. You will have command of that force, which will consist of the 11th brigade of your division, your brigade division, Royal Field artillery, and General Clery's division complete, and all the mounted troops, except 400.
4. You will of course act as circumstances require, but my idea is that you should continue throughout reusing your right, and throwing your left forward till you gain the open plain north of Spion Kop. Once there, you will command the rear of the position facing Potgieter's Drift, and, I think, render it untenable.
5. At Potgieter's there will be the 4th brigade, part of the 10th brigade, one battery Royal Field artillery, one Howitzer battery, two 4.7in. Naval guns. With them I shall threaten both the positions in front of us, and also attempt a crossing at Skiet's Drift, so as to hold the enemy off you as much as possible.
6. It is difficult to ascertain the numbers of the enemy with any sort of exactness. I do not think that there can be more than 400 on your left, and I estimate the total force that will be opposed to us about 7,000. I think they have only one or, at most, two guns.
7. You will take 2 ½ days' supply in your regimental transport, and a supply column holding one more. This will give you four days' supply, which should be enough. Every extra wagon is a great impediment.
8. I gathered that you did not want an ammunition column. I think myself that I should be inclined to take one column for the two brigade divisions. You may find a position on which it is expedient to expend a great deal of ammunition.

Warren's column comprised 529 officers, 14,853 other ranks, 4,856 horses (riding and draught), 36 15-pounder guns and 14 machine guns. Each battalion was restricted to three wagons: one for the troops' greatcoats, another to carry one day's rations, and the third for the officers' 20lb kits. The troops were in light marching order, each man carrying a day's 'emergency' ration, 150 rounds of ammunition, and, strapped to their belts, a jersey and a waterproof sheet.

An intelligence officer with the 16th Lancers, attached to Lord Dundonald's brigade to the extreme left of Buller's flank, reported seeing the enemy setting up gun positions in between Bastion Hill and Spioen Kop. Buller, however, did not believe that this was enough for him to waver from his overall plan. Warren, however, was greatly concerned that his force was going to meet strong Boer resistance once he crossed at Trichardt's. His apprehension was well-founded, as from their lofty positions while watching the cumbersome preparations of the British, the Boers significantly bolstered their positions

The formidable Spioenkop, Natal, Anglo-Boer War. (Photo Joanna Neal)

overlooking the drift. The topography facing Warren was as forbidding. To his west, Tabanyama rose 600ft above the plain, before dipping slightly and rising to the regular steep-sided Bastion Hill. To the east of this feature, a long, narrow spur ran southwards to Fairview Farm. The eastern sides of the spur dropped sharply into an immense chasm, surmounted by a deeply recessed triple re-entrant. There was then a more ragged south-jutting spur running down from Green Hill. Water courses dissected the spur nearer to the Tugela, giving rise to the lower elevations named Three Tree Hill and Picquet Hill. This whole terrain, which was about to become very familiar to 1/Yorks, was in plain sight of the Boer positions above.

At 2 am on the 17 January, Warren's column arrived on high ground above Trichardt's Drift, where the force bivouacked. Six Royal Field Artillery batteries, battling with mist that had enveloped the drift, took up their positions guarding the crossing. The Tugela was 80yd wide and flowing swiftly within 30ft-high stone banks. The 17th Royal Engineers constructed two pontoon bridges, with one specifically for the wagons.

Late that afternoon, the infantry crossed to the northern bank. Based on the certainty that the enemy was holding the heights from Bastion Hill all the way east to Spioen Kop, Woodgate's 11th Brigade, supported by Hart's 5th, immediately struck northwards, aiming for the water courses on either side of Picquet Hill, about 2,000yd away. At last light, and having met no resistance, the brigades halted in the foothills to overnight. The 1/Yorks was the most northerly unit, encamped on a slight rise with battalions from the Lancashire Fusiliers, Border Regiment and the Royal Dublin Fusiliers to their rear.

Warren's foothold that night and his ability over the next few days to turn the Boer right flank became even more imperative, as news had come through from the beleaguered

THE DEMAND FOR MORE TROOPS

Mr. Winston Spencer Churchill takes the occasion of General Buller's success to review the situation. In a telegram to the "Morning Post" he says:

Our late successes should not induce the Government to relax its military preparations. The principle of any scheme must be to manufacture soldiers, and as quickly as possible form them into divisions and ship them to Africa. It would be a fatal policy merely to keep the Field Army up to its present strength by providing a great reservoir in England. Soldiers are wanted in South Africa, and not at Aldershot.

The first object of everyone is to bring this horrible war to an end, and the shortest way is to pour a continual stream of men, guns, and supplies into the Cape, so that the Boer Republics are not only exposed to the beating of waves, but also to the force of a rising tide. Meanwhile there are many encouraging signs that the Boers are wearying of the struggle in ever-diminishing strength against ever-increasing odds. The sky already brightens with the promise of victorious peace.

St James's Gazette, Thursday, 22 February 1900

British troops in a holding position, Natal, Anglo-Boer War. (Photo Joanna Neal)

Ladysmith that disease was decimating the British garrison's strength – 2,400 troops were in hospital. There was, however, little that could be done to speed up the progress of the logistics wagon train over the Tugela. At 10 pm on the 18th, twenty-six hours after the first, the final wagon finally inched its way across the pontoon bridge to the north bank.

During the day, only Warren's cavalry had been active, scouting off to the west with their commander, Dundonald. In an ensuing engagement with a Boer outpost at Venter's Spruit near Acton Homes, and a misleading report from Dundonald, Warren returned 500 men of the Royal Dragoons to Dundonald – men Warren badly needed to guard his column's 15,000 oxen. Warren sent back a message to Dundonald ordering him to break off his engagement and retire to base, unless he was certain of success.

Not hearing from Dundonald and fearing for his left flank, at 6 am on the 19th, Warren reluctantly and knowingly compromised the essential strength of his force to determine Dundonald's fate by despatching General Sir Reginald Hildyard's 2nd Brigade to 'rescue' Dundonald. In ten hours, however, Hildyard's column had only moved two miles, his wagons, travelling in six parallel columns, almost totally unable to traverse the broken terrain.

At this time, having been static for thirty-six hours, Woodgate and Hart were ordered west towards Dundonald's position to the east of Venter's Spruit. Woodgate moved along the lower slopes of Tabanyama, guarding the column's right flank. That night, the brigade halted on Fairview Farm, the 1/Yorks and 2/Lancs securing the front, with three companies of the 2nd Devonshire to the rear. Three batteries – 19th, 28th and 63rd – of the Royal Field Artillery were in support of the position.

At a council of war with his senior commanders, Warren tabled his immediate strategy: clear the southern crest of Tabanyama of the enemy, extending from Bastion Hill to Three Tree Hill. This would then allow the Royal Field Artillery to set up forward positions from which to shell Green Hill and its eastern neighbour, Spioen Kop. It fell on 1/Yorks and 2/Lancs to take the western flank of Three Tree Hill on the Fairview Farm spur. Albeit that Buller had given Warren the authority to make his own decisions, he would remain critical of what he deemed to be Warren's failure to take the Boer line head on.

The artillery could not fit all six batteries onto Three Tree Hill, so the 78th, 28th and 19th batteries were posted to the east below Picquet Hill. All positions, however, were wholly unsatisfactory, with only the latter able to direct a fire on Spioen Kop, but only then at a steep upward angle.

At 9 am on the 20th, Hart moved his brigade westwards, above Venter's Spruit and closer to Bastion Hill. As he moved to the left, he absorbed Woodgate's two battalions, the 1/Yorks and 2/Lancs. With 1/Borders and the 2nd Dublin Fusiliers in support, 1/Yorks took the left and 2/Lancs the right, as the four battalions pressed forward in extended line up the spurs separating Bastion and Three Tree hills. Motivated by a desire to avenge the Colenso disaster, the troops surged forward at a brisk pace, all the while selecting advantage points whence to move on the enemy.

As quickly as they had set off, however, the British troops ran into a hail of Boer rifle and artillery fire. Undeterred, Hart's men took the enemy trenches on the southern crest of

Boer trenches, Natal, Anglo-Boer War. (Photo Joanna Neal)

Tabanyama, only to be ordered to halt by Clery, the latter fearful that a full-frontal pursuit of the fleeing enemy would result in failure. Elsewhere, Warren issued orders for Dundonald to secure the left flank of Bastion Hill from an enemy concentration on the Acton Homes road.

On the eventful day, in the Acton Homes area 1/Yorks sustained nine casualties, including seven killed. In their uphill assault on the Boer lines, the battalion had sixty-three men wounded, but, remarkably, only one died. Over the next three days, the 1/Yorks edged closer to the eastern slopes of Bastion Hill, part of a line held by the British in the shadow of the Tabanyama range.

On the 22nd, Warren turned his attention to Spioen Kop, believing that the capture of the imposing hill would guarantee a successful outcome of the battle. Warren called on Woodgate and his 11th Brigade to conduct the assault. Looking at his four Lancashire and Yorkshire battalions as he compiled his force, fate determined that 1/Yorks would not be selected by the general. Elements of their three sister battalions, however, would meet their fateful destiny in the bloody massacre at the hands of the Boers on the morning of 24 January 1900.

Brigade Orders by Major-General Woodgate, 23rd January, 1900.
1. The General Officer Commanding has decided to seize Spion Kop this night.
2. The following troops will compose this force:
   Royal Lancaster regiment (6 companies)
   2nd Lancashire Fusiliers
   Thorneycroft's Mounted Infantry (180 men)
   Half company 17th company Royal Engineers
   [Two companies South Lancashire joined after this order]

3. The above troops will rendezvous at White's Farm [Wright's Farm on the map] about half mile north-west of Pontoon Bridge [Trichardt's Drift] at 7 p.m.
4. Extra ammunition will be carried on the mules supplied by the 10th brigade.
5. One day's complete rations will be carried. Wagons with supplies and great-coats will be brought up as soon as possible without exposure; also water carts and machine guns.
6. The South Lancashire regiment will hand over six mules, three to each battalion, for water-carrying purposes.
7. Pack mules will be utilised for carrying water in waterproof sheets.
8. Twenty picks and twenty shovels to be carried in regulation stretchers.
9. Password, "Waterloo."

Of the total force that stormed Spioen Kop that day, 68 officers and 976 other ranks were killed. Late that night, the exhausted, parched and totally dispirited British troops relinquished Spioen Kop, leaving their dead and wounded behind.

Buller gave up on this costly attempt to reach Ladysmith, and by the 27th, the last of his troops had been withdrawn from Three Tree Hill. Buller was already looking at Vaal Krantz east of Spioen Kop for his next bid to reach Ladysmith. Withdrawing his troops south of the Tugela, Buller dismantled the pontoon bridge at Trichardt's Drift while concentrating his force on and around Zwart Kop for the assault on Commandant Ben Viljoen's commandos on Vaal Krantz.

Hauling a field piece up a rocky kopje, Natal, Anglo-Boer War. (Photo Joanna Neal)

AFTER SPION KOP

BULLER'S SECRET MOVEMENTS

After the failure of the second attempt to force the way to Ladysmith Sir Redvers Buller withdrew his entire force to the south bank of the Tugela. The morale of the men was not in any way shaken, and everyone was anxious for the renewed advance which was generally believed to be pending.

Indeed General Buller was reported to have said, in addressing his men, that the hard work which they had performed had not been in vain, that they had, in fact, gained the key of the road to Ladysmith, and that he hoped to reach the besieged town within a week's time.

The special correspondent of the *Daily Telegraph* sent the following message from Spearman's Camp:

'We experienced brilliant weather again to-day. There has been no cannonading here, and beyond a little sniping on the part of the Boers yesterday and to-day from the dongas and rocks east of Brakfontein, towards Skiet Drift, all has been quiet, our infantry lining the low, detached ridges on the north bank of Potgieter's Drift, and a few dismounted cavalrymen from the vicinity of Swarts Kop went forward, met, and quite held the enemy's snipers.

'Slight shelling of Ladysmith continues, but the damage done is trifling. Messages were freely interchanged between General Buller's and General White's camps by night with the calcium signal lamps, and by day with the heliograph. Ladysmith has two heliographs, and they are both working to-day, one from a point at Waggon Hill and the other from Thornton's Farm, near the Free State railway junction. The Boers, by means of their acetylene search and signal lights, tried ineffectually to blur the transmission of our signals. The men are enthusiastic at the prospect of a speedy advance.'

West Somerset Free Press, Saturday, 10 February 1900

To protect his left flank, Buller retained a bridgehead force at The Kopjes to the north of Potgieter's Drift. Two great loops of the Tugela provided natural barriers to the west, south and east. Abreast, the 1/Yorks and 1/S. Lancs – relieving the 4th Brigade during the night of the 4th – faced the open north, with the 2/KORL in support to their immediate rear. Behind this defensive position, seven batteries of the Royal Field Artillery, including the 61st Howitzer, not only bolstered the defensive line, but would provide a large-scale feint to draw the enemy over to his right.

At this time, commander of the 11th Brigade, Major General Woodgate, badly wounded on Spioen Kop, had been replaced by Major General Arthur Wynne. Woodgate died of his head wound in Mooi River Hospital on 23 March.

On the night of the 4th, Buller's main attack force was consolidating its launch positions at the bases of Zwart Kop and Mount Alice, ready for the diversionary actions to their west at first light.

At 6 am on the 5th, Wynne emerged from The Kopjes with his brigade, striking northwest in the direction of Brakfontein in an attempt to dupe the Boers that they were spearheading a major attack. The 1/Yorks and 2/KORL led from the left and right. The seven Royal Field Artillery batteries provided a barrage of deafening cover to the advancing infantry.

However, not even a single discharge from a Boer Mauser challenged Wynne's men. Behind Brakfontein's crest, the Senekal, Vrede and Free State commandos silently lay in their trenches as British shells churned up Brakfontein, following their commander, General Prinsloo's orders not to fire until the British infantry was within 400yd.

At 11.45 am, with the 11th Brigade now only 1,000yd from the Boer line, three Boer guns and a pom-pom opened fire on the exposed artillery. The infantry immediately halted and lay down, now very curious as to why there was still no rifle fire levelled against them. Casualties were slight.

At 12.20 pm, fire from 28th Battery was redirected away from Brakfontein towards Vaal Krantz. The other batteries followed soon after, leaving only the 7th Battery to cover Wynne's withdrawal when the time came.

At 1.30 pm, Wynne, considering his diversionary task a success, called on his troops to withdraw. As the 11th Brigade got to their feet and turned about, Prinsloo's men could

Base camp hospital, Ladysmith during the siege. (Photo Joanna Neal)

remain patient no longer, and enfiladed the retiring brigade. The 1/Yorks then suffered its highest number of fatal casualties of Buller's Ladysmith campaign. Nine men were either killed on the spot or succumbed to their wounds on that day. A further fourteen sustained wounds. Two days later, Buller gave up on any chance of taking Vaal Krantz. On 11 February, 1/Yorks was detached from 11th Brigade, with 2/Lancs the following day. The battalion was retired to Chievely, south of Colenso, but on the 27th, the men were recalled and were back in the drive to Ladysmith, positioned only nine miles from Ladysmith. Lieutenant Colonel Frederick Kitchener had replaced the wounded Wynne as commander of the 11th Brigade.

On 3 March, 1/Yorks participated in the triumphant procession into Ladysmith.

Battle of the Somme, 1 July 1916

No splendid rite is here – yet lay him low,
Ye comrades of his youth he fought beside,
Close where the winds do sigh and wild flowers grow
Where the sweet brook doth babble by his side.
No splendour, yet we lay him tenderly
To rest, his requiem in artillery.

'A Soldier's Funeral', Company Sergeant John Streets, D Company,
12th Sheffield City Battalion, York and Lancaster Regiment,
missing in action 1 July 1916 and never seen alive again.

In August 1914, the newly appointed Minister of War, Lord Herbert Kitchener, requested and received parliamentary authority to recruit 500,000 soldiers, together with a vote of £100,000,000 to pay for what became known as Kitchener's New Army. His first appeal went out at the end of the month, seeking volunteers from the heavily populated industrialized midland and northern counties. This gave rise to a popular phenomenon in which men from the same club, association, place of work, and towns and cities, would enlist on the basis that they would serve together – 'Pals' battalions were born.

The 12th (Service) Battalion (Sheffield), York & Lancaster Regiment (12/Yorks) was one such Pals battalion. Officially raised on 10 September 1914, by December, the battalion strength stood at 1,130 officers and other ranks. Brigaded into the 94th with Accrington Pals from the East Lancashire Regiment and two sister Barnsley Pals' battalions from the York and Lancaster Regiment, the brigade combined with the 92nd and 93rd brigades, and the 21 West Yorkshire Pioneers, to form a New Army 31st Division, commanded by Major General Robert Wanless-O'Gowan. The 31st, in turn, was amalgamated with two regular divisions, the 4th and 29th, and the Territorial Army 48th (South Midland) Division, to form VIII Corps under Lieutenant-General Aylmer Hunter-Weston, a part of General Sir Henry Rawlinson's Fourth Army. This would be the order of battle in which the Sheffield City Pals found themselves on the Western Front on 1 July 1916.

Men of the York and Lancaster Regiment training at trench digging, Redmires, 1915.

FAR-REACHING CHARACTER OF THE BOMBARDMENT

SHELLS BURSTING IN BATTALIONS

British Headquarters in France, June 27

It certainly cannot be said that things have been 'quiet' upon the Western Front during the last two days. The British artillery has been boisterous at many points of the line.

Yesterday I was in the Loos salient, and the rattle and boom of the guns was practically ceaseless. Nor was the uproar constant in any one particular spot, but seemed to fade away, so to express it, thus indicating the far-reaching character of the bombardment.

As I write my ears are still ringing with the resonance of our guns along a sector reaching well down towards the Somme which I visited this afternoon. As far as the eye can reach – and this from a capital vantage point was a good many leagues – the line of the enemy trenches was traced by the sullen-looking puffs of high explosive projectiles, bursting 'not singly but in battalions.

Birmingham Mail, Thursday, 29 June 1916

The months following the battalion's formation was filled with diverse and intense military training, ranging from weapons handling to trench digging. During this period, Commanding Officer Lieutenant Colonel C. Mainwaring retired, unfit for active service. In September 1915, Lieutenant Colonel J. A. Crosthwaite assumed command.

On 21 December, the 12/Yorks embarked on the SS *Nestor* from Devonport, the Middle East their first theatre of war. In the wake of the disastrous Gallipoli campaign, the battalion, as part of the 31st Division, performed defensive duties in the northern-most of three zones along the Suez Canal, an area stretching from the Mediterranean to the El Ferdan station. Battalion headquarters was set up at Port Said on the Mediterranean. On 11 March 1916, the HMT *Briton* transported the battalion to France, sailing into Marseilles five days later.

At the end of 1915, veteran of the South African campaign, Lieutenant General Sir Douglas Haig replaced Lieutenant General Sir John French as Commander-in-Chief of British forces in France. The new incumbent, fully cognizant of the enormous pressures placed on his predecessor to resign, immediately set about formulating ideas for a spring offensive on the Western Front. By February, Haig had become inclined towards a combined Anglo-French operation straddling the River Somme employing around twenty-five divisions. Sufficiently confident of the concept, Haig tasked newly promoted commander of the Third Army, Lieutenant General Edmund Allenby, and Lieutenant General Sir Henry Rawlinson, commander of the Fourth, to attach body to his framework.

At Gallipoli, 1915.

Lying roughly east–west, the great bend of the Upper Somme and its western tributary at Thiepval, the Ancre, intersect a rolling tableland criss-crossed by a myriad of small streams and dotted with dozens of hamlets and villages. The Somme meanders considerably, and nowhere does the terrain rise above 500ft. As a consequence, poplar-lined, elevated Roman roads provided the chief landmarks. To the north of the Somme above the Frise Valley, an undulating plain rises to a ridge 300ft above the Somme, marked by the towns of Guillemont, Longueval, Bazentin le Petit, Poziéres and Thiepval. From here, high ground stretches northwards through Beaucourt, Hébuterne, Gommecourt and Fonquevillers.

Up to the summer of 1916, there had been little activity on the Picardy front, which encompasses the Somme department. Since July the previous year, the British had taken over and held most of the line from Arras to the Somme, but, apart from occasional small-scale raids and localized artillery bombardments, the situation was static.

Across no man's land, the Germans held much of the high ground from Arras southwards. The German front was characterized by strong front positions, with firing, support and reserve trenches and a sophisticated labyrinth of deep dugouts and bunkers. A second line, similar in strength to the first, lay behind an intermediate line covering the artillery batteries. Farther back there were fortified woods and villages linked with trenches to facilitate third and fourth lines. The strength of the German front was greatly enhanced by a strong network of logistical support railways.

Early in April, plans were submitted to general headquarters in which Rawlinson stressed that limited resources at their disposal would not allow for a front wider than 20,000yd, and a maximum depth of 5,000yd. He was also adamant that a sustained, methodical artillery bombardment, lasting forty-eight to seventy-two hours, would destroy German wire obstacles and neutralize the machine guns guarding the approaches to their trenches. If this worked, he believed the rest would be easy.

In preparatory deployments, the VIII Corps faced a front from the village of Serre in the north, to the northern outskirts of Beaumont Hamel. The German first line ran from an eastern spur of Auchonvillers, through Y Ravine to Hawthorne Ridge, across Beaumont Hamel valley and Beaucourt spur, before traversing a series of ridges and depressions to Grandcourt spur on which Serre stood. In the northern sector, allocated to the 31st Division, no man's land was 200yd wide and largely void of cover. The 94th Brigade was deployed to the northern extremity of the British first line for the assault on 1 July.

On 24 June, known as U-Day, the British bombardment of the German line began, accompanied by heavy discharges of gas. The next day, the trial registering of the new siege guns began. Heavy gunfire continued into the night, assisting a series of ten raiding parties to break into German trenches and take prisoners. At first light, the bombardment from the Royal Garrison Artillery recommenced, at the rate of 250,000 shells a day. This was, however, still only a demonstration by Haig while the batteries zeroed in on intended targets. On 27 June, the area between the Ancre and the Somme was selected as the chief demonstration point, ultimately giving way the following day to the start of the main bombardment.

Field kitchens, the Somme. (Photo IWM)

All the while, the German guns remained largely and uncharacteristically silent, giving rise, as it turned out, to a false sense that the British guns were dominating the battlefield and successful in their objectives.

At dawn on 1 July, hundreds of quick-firing Stokes mortars augmented the 25-mile-wide artillery barrage with a rate of fire of thirty rounds a minute. For the 94th Brigade, as zero hour approached, the German line to their front was the most prepared. At 7.20 am, elements from two of the brigade's battalions, the 12/Yorks and 11/E. Lancs, leapt out their trenches and started filtering through their own wire to lie down and wait in no man's land for the main attack at 7.30 am. They ran straight into heavy German machine-gun fire that was accompanied by heavy artillery from Puisieux and field-gun fire around Serre.

At zero hour, 144,000 infantry troops of the British Fourth Army clambered over their parapets. The 94th and 93rd brigades stormed in the direction of the German trenches in front of Serre, while 92nd Brigade were held in reserve in their trenches. At the end of that first day of slaughter, they had not moved from their trenches.

For 12/Yorks in the Colincamps sector, the night of 30 June was long and sleepless. According to the battalion war diary, at 1.40 am on 1 July, senior officers of the battalion arrived at John Copse. Acting commanding officer, Major A. Plackett (Lieutenant Colonel Crosthwaite had been taken to hospital the previous day), his second-in-command

Major A. R. Hoette, adjutant Captain N. L. Tunbridge, signalling officer Lieutenant H. Oxley, and other members of headquarters staff found that A and C companies had not yet arrived at the staging trenches parallel with no man's land. In the brigade sector, there were four copses, named after the four Gospels of the New Testament. From north to south, they were John, Luke, Mark and Matthew. John and Luke copses fronted the first line of 12/Yorks, named Copse Trench.

At 1.55 am, Captain Clarke reported that his party had successfully cut the British wire on their front, and had, by 12.30 am, finished the laying of tapes on the battalion front.

The first and second waves from A Company were reported at 2.40 am to be in position, ready in assembly trenches Copse and Rob Roy respectively. Company headquarters had been set up at the junction of Jordan communication trench and Copse Trench.

At 3.45 am, in spite of a report from an officer that the whole battalion was in position in their assembly trenches, direct confirmation had only been received from A Company at Luke Copse. Five minutes later, D Company reported that they were in their designated position in New Cut to the north-west of Touvent Farm and adjacent to the fourth wave Monk Trench. The other two companies were, however, now in position, having been significantly delayed by flooded communications trenches Northern Avenue, Pylon and Nairne. C Company was ready at John Copse in the first wave Copse Trench, and B Company to the rear in third wave Campion Trench.

Setting up a 15in. howitzer on the Somme, July 1916. (Photo IWM)

FIERCE BATTLES ON THE SOMME

STRONG GERMAN POSTS TAKEN

Long-awaited news of a great British offensive reached London on Saturday morning in a terse report from Headquarters. An attack has been launched north of the River Somme at 7.30 that morning; British troops had broken into the German forward system of defences on a front of 16 miles, and a French attack on our right was proceeding equally satisfactorily.

The British attack was on a front of 20 miles in the country of chalk downs and woods on either side of the Ancre and to the north of the Somme.

The battle line to the east of Albert curved sharply into the Somme Valley, making a great salient with its point at Fricourt. It was in this salient that we won our greatest successes on Saturday. Late in the evening Headquarters reported that we had captured the German labyrinth of trenches here on a front of seven miles and that the strongly fortified villages of Montauban, of especial importance, and Mametz were in our possession, while Fricourt, which eventually fell on Sunday, was threatened.

Everywhere the battle was intense. In the centre, where earlier in the day unofficial news had come through that our troops had taken Serre and La Boiselle, the Headquarters report said the struggle was still severe and that we had gained many strong points.

In the north, to beyond Gommecourt, the day had not gone quite so well, and we had been unable to retain portions of ground gained in our first attack.

Warwick and Warwickshire Advertiser, Saturday, 8 July 1916

At 4.05 am, German artillery started homing in on John Copse and the front line. A period of some confusion ensued, culminating in a report being received at 6 am from C Company saying that British artillery was dropping short into the battalion line between John and Luke copses. With a failure in communications, a runner was immediately despatched to brigade to inform them of the unfolding tragedy in their own lines. Half an hour later, C Company reported that they had sustained fourteen casualties, including eight killed, mainly from 12 Platoon. Brigade responded by messaging C Company to tell them that nothing could immediately be done about the 'friendly-fire', and that they should report again at 7 am. Mercifully, shelling by their own guns had ceased and no more casualties were reported.

Taking stock as zero hour approached, Brigade, now totally reliant on runners for communication, discovered that the front line and Copse Trench had sustained considerable damage from the persistent German shelling, while Monk and Campion trenches were very heavy going as a result of the atrocious weather.

German artillery, Western Front. (Photo City of Toulouse Archives)

It was very apparent to Brigade that the reason behind the heavy German bombardment was largely attributable to the yawning and very visible gaps that had been cut in the British wire to allow infantry to pass through unhindered towards the German lines. This, together with the sight at first light of lines of tape emanating from the British lines, unwittingly gave the Germans several hours' notice of the intended British assault. In fact, at 3.30 am that morning, the German 52nd Division headquarters sent a despatch to the 169th Regiment at Serre to expect a British assault at 4.30 am. All they had wrong was the time, but they had erred in their favour. It is also believed that the detonation of the now famous gigantic mine under Hawthorne Ridge at 7.20 am gave the Germans a valuable ten-minute advantage in which to ready themselves.

At 7.20 am, the first wave, from A and C companies, and under cover from artillery and mortars, moved about 100yd into no man's land, where they took to the ground. The second wave followed nine minutes later, dropping down 30yd behind their comrades of the first wave. At the same time, the third and fourth waves left Campion and Monk trenches to move forward in single-file sections. German artillery now concentrated on Monk, slowly rolling forward to the British front line.

Zero hour – 7.30 am, the British artillery lifted and the first two waves in no man's land got up and commenced with their role in the attack. Half of C Company in the first wave was immediately mowed down by the Germans who had come out from the shelter of their underground dugouts as soon as the British guns stopped firing. Company commander, C Company, Captain William Arthur Colley died instantly when hit by a shell. An intact body was never found, so the 47-year-old officer from Sheffield is memorialized on the Thiepval Memorial. Realizing that they were not facing an attack, German sections to the north of Serre diverted their fire at the left flank of the advancing 12/Yorks.

A Company also lost their commander, 24-year-old Captain William Spencley Clark, killed by machine-gun fire on the German wire. The Germans had six Maxim machine guns pointing at 94th Brigade.

The third and fourth waves, comprising B and D companies, had to start their advance much father back as Rob Roy Trench had been demolished by German shelling. As they cleared their holding trenches, there was no cover, and they lost half their strength by the time they reached no man's land, also falling to the enemy's machine guns. Whole sections were obliterated. At around 10.30 am, Major Hoette was wounded while at his station in John Copse. Two and a half hours later, battalion headquarters moved to Mark Copse to make way for the flood of wounded arriving at John Copse. No reports had yet been received from any of the companies. A small number of troops from A and C companies succeeded in making it into German trenches to the right of the assault, but elsewhere, the Sheffield Pals found the German wire intact – untouched by British artillery. While a few found relative shelter in shell holes, the rest of the fully exposed troops were ripped apart by heavy rifle and machine-gun fire from the entrenched enemy. Wave upon wave, hour upon hour, the senseless slaughter continued, the wounded and dead from Sheffield piling up against the impenetrable German wire.

With darkness came relief for those still alive in no man's land. Stretcher bearers and medics stumbled into the night to recover whatever life they could. Those who were able crawled back to their line. In the brigade sector, able-bodied soldiers commenced clearing the trenches of casualties while repairing the trenches as best they could.

By 8 pm, reports started coming through: only a few battalion signallers and runners not wounded, Lewis machine-gun pan magazines completely run out ...

At 10 pm, Brigade sent in the 13th and 14th (Barnsley) service battalions, York and Lancaster Regiment (13/Yorks and 14/Yorks) to relieve the mauled 12/Yorks. The battalion would retire to Rolland Trench, its headquarters being set up in a deep sap (tunnel) off it. Later that night, unconfirmed reports indicated that about 150 troops, having managed to penetrate the German line opposite Mark Copse, were holding their position in the German front line. Battalion knew they had to be retrieved.

At 1.30 am in the morning of 2 July, 12/Yorks officers led two patrols from 14/Yorks to check if there were in fact any City Battalion soldiers stranded in German lines. All they encountered, however, were a few wounded men who stated that the German trenches were back under German control. Flares and sporadic machine-gun fire seemed to confirm what they had said. The patrols returned, bringing back with them any wounded men they found. Even after Corps declared no man's land clear on 4 July, survivors continued for some time to find their way back to relative safety.

VIII Corps sustained 14,000 casualties on 1 July, the worst of all the corps.

The City Battalion remained in the trenches until late on 3 July when, at 8 pm, the battalion was relieved by 1/4th Oxfordshire and Buckinghamshire Light Infantry from the 48th Division.

German trenches and wire defences under fire. (Photo Bundesarchiv)

Including the 80 reinforcements sent on the night of the 1st, a mere 202 shattered men remained to march away on the 4th from the carnage on the Somme. Twenty-two officers had participated in the attack – only four walked away with their men to Louvencourt. Coming as a final insult, the battalion then had to march twenty miles to Longuevillette, where, at 10 am on 7 July, the first opportunity finally arose to officially audit the battalion's latest strength. The roll call was pitiful. Of the 36 officers and 980 other ranks on 30 June, only 18 officers and 485 other ranks answered the call of their names. In less than a week, half the 12/Yorks had become casualty statistics, not including the 75 who were only slightly wounded and remained on duty.

Spread virtually evenly across the four companies, the roll call of other ranks at that particular point in time revealed:

Killed in action – 45
Died of wounds – 12
Wounded – 237
Missing – 201

Of the 201 listed as missing, all but eighteen were later confirmed dead. The corpses were to lie and rot in no man's land until the following spring when the Germans were pushed back to the Hindenburg Line.

Of the 248 all ranks that lost their lives on the Somme on 1 July 1916 a staggering 165 were never identified or found. Their remains may still be scattered across the overgrown battlefield or interred as body parts, their Commonwealth War Graves Commission Portland headstone carrying the simple yet poignant epitaph: 'A Soldier of the Great War – Known Unto God'. Their names are inscribed on the Thiepval Memorial on the Ancre, together with the other 73,000 British soldiers who died on the Somme and whose bodies were never found.

The remnants of the battalion was strengthened again and continued to serve in France, until 2 February 1918 when, while still in France, the 94th Brigade was disbanded, and with it, the 12th (Service) Battalion (Sheffield), York & Lancaster Regiment.

Europe, April 1944–April 1945

The Hallamshires, first raised in 1859 as the Hallamshire Rifles, had, by the time of the Second World War, established an outstanding record of volunteer service. The unit saw action in the Anglo-Boer War of 1899–1902 and in the First World War, the latter bearing the title 4th (Hallamshire) Battalion, The York and Lancaster Regiment. Come the outbreak of hostilities in Europe in 1939, the '4th' had been dropped from the battalion's title, and they became known simply as The Hallamshires. During the war, the battalion would sustain 847 casualties and earn twenty-seven decorations, including a Victoria Cross.

Early in 1940, troops from Berwick-on-Tweed, Northumberland, Durham, Yorkshire, Lincolnshire, Rutland, Leicestershire, Nottinghamshire and Derbyshire, provided the formation strength for the 49th (East Riding) Division, its headquarters at York. With its headquarters at Doncaster, one of the 49th's brigades was the 146th Infantry Brigade, comprising the Hallamshire Battalion, the York and Lancaster Regiment, 4th Battalion,

---

ALLIES WILL GIVE FULL AID TO INVADED NORWAY

BRITISH FORCE REPORTED TO BE ON THE WAY

Reports that a British expeditionary force is on the way to Norway have been received in New York, according to the Columbia Broadcasting System.

Britain and France are to go to the help of Norway, which with Denmark, was invaded by Germany to-day. After a meeting of cabinet ministers at 10, Downing Street this morning the following statement was issued by the Foreign Office:

'His Majesty's Government and the French Government have at once assured the Norwegian Government that in view of the German invasion of their country, they have decided forthwith to extend their full aid to Norway and have intimated that they will fight the war in full association with them.

'The necessary naval and military steps are accordingly being taken in conjunction with the French.'

Lancashire Evening Post, Tuesday, 9 April 1940

Lincolnshire Regiment, 1/4th Battalion, King's Own Yorkshire Light Infantry and the 146th Infantry Brigade Anti-Tank Company.

The 146th Brigade's first war deployment was to Norway 10 April 1940, as part of the Anglo-French Mauriceforce group. Under the command of Major General Adrian Carton de Wiart VC, the 146th element of the force went ashore at Namsos in Central Norway on the 14th, while the French half-brigade landed five days later. The German 181st Division and the Luftwaffe, however, ensured that the Allied campaign in Central Norway lasted only a fortnight. On 2 May, Mauriceforce was evacuated from Namsos.

Commanding officer of the Hallamshires, Lieutenant Colonel C. G. Robins, together with Captain W. L. Cave, went ashore the following morning to check that no one had been left behind from the previous night. At 9.30 am, they turned their backs on mountains of stores and scores of vehicles in the deserted town, and boarded the destroyer HMS *Afridi*, where they joined forty-seven other officers and ranks from the battalion – the rest had embarked on transporters.

As everyone had expected, the Luftwaffe arrived over the convoy to bomb and strafe, specifically targeting the escort destroyers. The large French Guépard-class destroyer *Bison* was the first to be hit, sinking in less than thirty minutes and taking 136 French sailors down with her. The *Afridi* hove to, to pick up 136 survivors from the dangerously cold water.

British troops sift through the ruins of Namsos in Norway after a German air raid, April 1940. (Photo Capt Keating)

Afridi now sped to catch up to the convoy, but at 1 pm, as she got closer, she came under a heavy German attack. Hit just forward of the bridge, the Tribal-class destroyer went down in twenty minutes. The Hallamshire contingent on board were having a meal in the forward mess at the time. The bomb penetrated the mess bulkhead, killing thirteen and injuring eleven others. Two other destroyers, HMS *Imperial* and *Griffin*, came alongside the *Afridi*, to allow Hallamshire and naval survivors to safely jump off the doomed vessel. Thirty-five French crew members rescued when the *Bison* went down also perished.

Forty-eight hours after their departure from Norway, all British troops arrived back at Scapa Flow. Here, the Hallamshires were transferred to the SS *Duchess of Athol*, which sailed for Glasgow. Upon disembarkation, the battalion were garrisoned at Stobs Camp, near Hawick in Scotland.

In London, the ramifications of this ignominious evacuation from Europe and failing to stand by her allies on the continent, had immediate and far-reaching consequences. The political corridors of Westminster reverberated with recriminations and blame-seeking. Winston Churchill in his *The Second World War: The Gathering Storm* (Bantam, London, 1961), was his usual verbose self:

> The many disappointments and disasters of the brief campaign in Norway caused profound perturbation at home, and the currents of passion mounted even in the breasts of some of those who had been most slothful and purblind in the years before the war. The Opposition called for a debate on the war situation, and this was arranged for May 7. The House was filled with members in a high state of irritation and distress. Mr Chamberlain's opening statement did not stem the hostile tide. He was mockingly interrupted and reminded of his speech on April 4, when in quite another connection he had cautiously said, 'Hitler missed the bus.'

On 10 May, Prime Minister Neville Chamberlain resigned and the king invited Winston Churchill to form a new government.

Britain now faced greater isolation, against a hostile German front that stretched from the northern reaches of Norway to the Franco-Spanish border. In the vast expanses of the frigid North Sea, German *unterseeboot* – U-boat – submarines, often with Luftwaffe support preyed heavily on Allied shipping.

Realizing that the loss of Iceland would sever Britain's remaining lifeline to the east, in June the 49th Division was deployed to prevent German invasion. At the end of the month, the Hallamshires arrived in Iceland with the balance of the 146th Infantry Brigade. The battalion and the Lincolns established their bases in the barren, sparsely populated town of Akureyri in the north.

Covering an area of 150 square miles, their time was spent learning to ski while undergoing winter warfare training. They learned to build igloos and how to scale vertical rock faces.

After an uneventful two-year tour of duty, the battalion returned to England in the summer of 1942, where Leominster in Herefordshire became their home for the next year.

Badges of the York and Lancaster Regiment

York and Lancaster Regiment
cap badge (with lugs)
1889–1914

84th Foot
Shako plate

York and Lancaster Regiment
cap badge (brass cast)
1940s

General Service
button
1890s

York and Lancaster Regiment
shoulder title
1940s-1950s

York and Lancaster Regiment
button
1900–1958

York and Lancaster Regiment
collar badge
1889–1958

49th (West Riding) Division
shoulder patch worn during World War Two

York and Lancaster Regiment
cap badge (with slider)
1914–1958

York and Lancaster Regiment
shoulder title
1890s–1940s

Yorkshire Brigade
cap badge
1958–1968

Yorkshire Regiment
tactical recognition flash
2006 to date

Yorkshire Regiment
cap badge
2006 to date

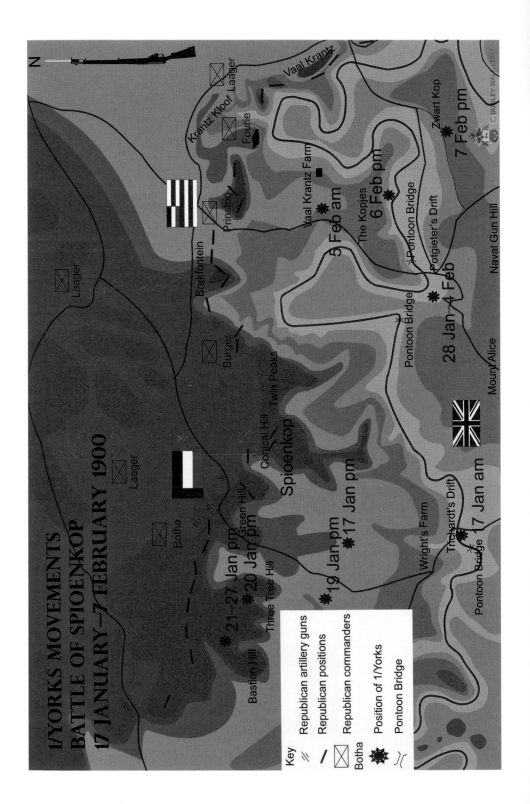

1/YORKS MOVEMENTS
BATTLE OF SPIOENKOP
17 JANUARY–7 FEBRUARY 1900

N

Laager

Laager

Botha

Three Tree Hill

21–27 Jan pm
20 Jan pm

Green Hill

Bastion Hill

Conical Hill

Twin Peaks

Spioenkop

19 Jan pm

17 Jan pm

Wright's Farm

Trichardt's Drift

Pontoon Bridge   17 Jan am

Mount Alice

Naval Gun Hill

Burger

Brakfontein

Prinsloo

Krantz Kloof

Laager

Fourie

Vaal Krantz

Vaal Krantz Farm

5 Feb am

The Kopjes

6 Feb pm

Pontoon Bridge

Potgieter's Drift

Zwart Kop

7 Feb pm

Pontoon Bridge

28 Jan–4 Feb

Key

⫽ Republican artillery guns

/ Republican positions

⊠ Botha Republican commanders

✸ Position of 1/Yorks

)(Pontoon Bridge

C DUDLEY WAL 2017

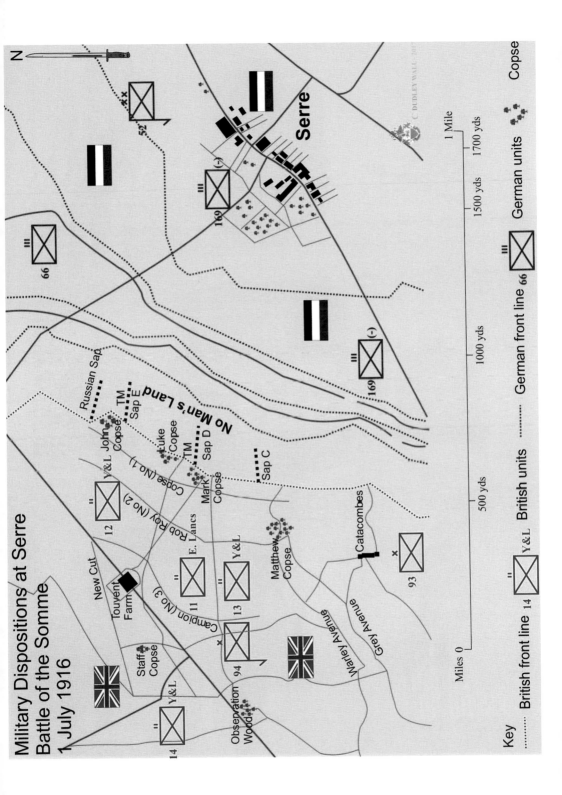

Military Dispositions at Serre
Battle of the Somme
1 July 1916

Serre

N

52
66
169 (-)
66
169 (-)

Russian Sap
John Copse
TM
Sap E
Luke Copse
Copse (No.1)
Mark Copse
TM
Sap D
Sap C

No Man's Land

Y&L
12
Rob Roy (No.2)
E. Lancs
11
Y&L
13
Matthew Copse
Catacombes
93

New Cut
Touvent Farm
Staff Copse
Campion (No.3)
Y&L
94
Warley Avenue
Grey Avenue

Y&L
14

Observation Wood

C. DUDLEY WALE 2017

Miles 0   500 yds   1000 yds   1500 yds   1 Mile
                                                   1700 yds

Key   ┈┈┈ British front line   14 Y&L British units   ┈┈┈ German front line   66 German units

           Y&L British units   German units   Copse

Uniforms and Accoutrements

Grenadier 65th Foot
1758

Shako
84th Foot

Private 84th Foot
1845

Shako
65th Foot

Regimetal drum
1st Y&L Regiment

Helmet
8th Bn West Riding of Yorkshire
Rifle Volunteers

Corporal
1st Bn Y&L
1900

Sergeant
12th Bn Y&L
1916

Private
4th Bn (Hallamshire) Y&L
1940

1st York and Lancaster Regiment (former 65th) fought at the Second Battle of El Teb on 29 February 1884, against a Mahdist Sudanese army led by Osman Digna.

The battalion then saw action at the Battle of Tamai, 13 March 1884, also against the Sudanese forces of Osman Digna.

Field Marshal Herbert Charles Onslow Plumer, 1st Viscount Plumer, GCB, GCMG, GCVO, GBE.

Medals L–R: Egypt Medal, British South Africa Company Medal, Queen's South Africa Medal, King's South Africa Medal, 1914–15 Star, British War Medal (1914–20), Victory War Medal (with MiD oak leaf), Queen Victoria Diamond Jubilee Medal, King Edward VII Coronation Medal, Turkish Order of Medjidie, Italian Bronze Medal for Military Valour, French Croix de Guerre, Belgian Croix de Guerre, Khedive's Star.

British Orders of Knighthood L–R: Knight Grand Cross of the Order of the Bath, Knight Grand Cross of the Order of St Michael and St George, Knight Grand Cross of the Royal Victorian Order, Knight Grand Cross of the Order of the British Empire. On the shoulder sash, The Knight of Grace of the Venerable Order of St John. (Photos Gerry van Tonder)

The Queen's Own Yorkshire Dragoons used vehicles such as the British Lloyd carrier in North Africa during the Second World War. (Photo Gerry van Tonder)

The Mastiff 3 protected patrol vehicle employed by British forces in Helmand, Afghanistan, including the Yorkshire Regiment.

Sheffield War Memorial. (Photo Gerry van Tonder)

6in. naval gun, Iceland, 1940. (Photo War Office)

In June 1943, the 49th Division moved to Scotland for 'special training', perceived by many to be a prelude to an invasion of Europe. Just before Christmas, the Hallamshires were moved to Hopton Camp, near Great Yarmouth. En route, the battalion was granted permission to exercise their right to march through Sheffield with fixed bayonets, pursuant to the York and Lancaster Regiment having been bestowed with the Freedom of the City the previous month.

Early in 1944, there was great disappointment when the 50th Division, fresh from its campaigns in the Western Desert and the invasion of Sicily and Italy, replaced the 49th as one of the D-Day invasion formations.

The day before the Normandy assault, the 146th Infantry Brigade found itself in a transit camp in Sussex, kitted up with full battle gear and awaiting deployment orders. On 10 June, LCIs (landing craft infantry) brought the battalion to the French beaches at Ver-sur-Mer, in the area of Gold Beach. By this time, the battalion's commanding officer was Lieutenant Colonel Trevor Hart Dyke, and the brigade formed part of XXX Corps.

The battalion first saw action on 14 June during the two-day clearance of the village of Audrieu, in which Lieutenant F. Tett became the battalion's first casualty when he was shot and killed by a German sniper. On the second day of the operation, A Company under Major R. I. Slater and with artillery support from the 69th Field regiment, took woods and orchards held by two companies of Germans to the east of the village. Lieutenant Joseph Arthur Noiseux, on attachment from the Royal Canadian Infantry Corps, was killed in the assault. Major P. S. Newton's D Company followed up with a bayonet charge to clear the objective.

The battalion's advance now stalled, as bad weather prevented them from receiving a replenishment of ammunition and rations. This time, however, was spent constructively.

Lieutenants (both acting majors) Leslie Lonsdale-Cooper (C Company) and John Nicholson (D Company) conducted night patrols to locate German positions, actions which would earn them both the Military Cross.

On 25 June, XXX Corps, broke south, where, twelve miles from the Normandy beaches, the 49th Division was tasked with taking Fontenay-le-Pesnel and high ground outside the village. The 146th Brigade would lead a two-battalion thrust to the west of the objective, the Hallamshires on the left and the 1/4th King's Own Yorkshire Light Infantry (4/KOYLI) to the right of the attack.

At first light, B and C companies advanced, while A and D remained in reserve. Low-lying mist, smoke from artillery fire, as well as that laid down by the enemy, reduced visibility to five yards. The inevitable confusion ensued, and in a short space of time, the two attacking companies had lost both their direction and contact with the various platoons. Accepting that the two companies engulfed in the mist and smoke would not be able to reach their objective across a stream, Lieutenant Colonel Hart Dyke sent in his two reserve companies, A and D. Eventually, and to the commanding officer's relief, elements of A and B companies crossed the stream and secured their objectives.

In the meantime, on the left flank, Lieutenant A. Cowell with one of the battalion's anti-tank guns engaged two advancing German Panther tanks. Cowell, however, only could only disable one enemy tank before his weapon was knocked out. Another gun was immediately and very courageously dragged into position by Lance Corporal Williams and, using the new sabot ammunition, the crew eliminated the second tank. Williams would receive the Military Medal for his actions, while the battalion received a £5 prize from the divisional commander for destroying the first Panther tank.

Troops of the 49th Division pass a disabled German Panther tank, Operation Epsom, Normandy, June 1944. (Photo Sgt Christie)

WEST FRONT IS NEARLY A CONTINUOUS LINE NOW

The Western Front is nearly established as a continuous line. This has been shown by reports from the battle front, from enemy sources, and from geographical features of the assault zone.

Focal points of this developing front are Caen, where there is an armoured battle in the area for possession of the town, and in which battle the British forces are making progress, and Carentan, for which the Germans are putting up a very determined resistance.

Allied strategical and tactical assaults have been limited, and we have reason to be very thankful that the air assault before and immediately after D-Day was on such a large scale.

Rommel has been severely handicapped in his conduct of the campaign because of it. He made rapid concentrations of his garrison troops and tactical reserves, and was called upon much earlier than he expected to deal with a break-through by Allied assault troops on the Western Wall. We scored a bull-point there.

Rommel's plan is to roll our forces up from Caen along the coast to the west. General Montgomery has dictated the terms of this battle; Rommel has set its course. Both sides will bring up fresh forces as soon as they are available.

Great praise is again due to the Navy and the Merchant Navy for maintaining disembarkation operations. We need bombing weather to pin down Rommel's air and land defences.

Gloucestershire Echo, Saturday, 10 June 1944

The 146th Infantry Brigade had met exceptionally heavy enemy resistance. After 4/KOYLI had advanced to clear Tessel Wood, the Hallamshires received orders not to leapfrog them to continue gaining ground. Consolidation of the Hallamshires was urgently required, which, under the adverse conditions that restricted effective communications and visibility, could only be achieved through face-to-face contact. Hart Dyke turned to his B Echelon, from which he assembled a ragtag group of rear echelon staff, including cooks and administrative staff, and personally led them out to find and re-assemble the left section of his battalion.

At Calvaire (Calvary), some 300yd to the rear of the Hallamshire's left flank, Hart Dyke found B Company dug in, having sustained heavy casualties that were officially given as 123. Company commander, 33-year-old Major David Eadon Lockwood was among the dead. He is interred in the St Manvieu War Cemetery near the village of Cheux, four miles east of Fontenay-le-Pesnel. Lieutenant Oliver Watson-Jones died later that day, the 25th, of his wounds, while Lieutenant Jack Firth died of his wounds on 1 July.

On 27 June, the attack was renewed, the Hallamshires tasked with taking the southern part of Tessel Wood, before leapfrogging sister battalions the Lincolns and 4/KOYLI to occupy the Vendes area, less than two miles to the south. However, the resistance from the Germans occupying Vendes was so fierce, that the attack stalled. The Hallamshires were ordered to remain at Tessel Wood, where they dug in for three weeks. They suffered further casualties from ongoing German mortaring and shelling.

Active patrolling continued during this static period. On 10 July, Major Nicholson took two platoons from A Company on a mission to capture a German soldier. In frantic hand-to-hand combat, in which fifteen German troops were killed, Nicholson was repelled, sustaining six dead, sixteen wounded and three missing. Lieutenant Harry Edward Poynor was among those killed.

Frustration and anger grew in the Supreme Headquarters Allied Expeditionary Force as Supreme Commander US General Dwight D. Eisenhower became critical of Montgomery's inability to breakout from the Normandy bridgehead to take the strategically important town of Caen. As commander of the 21st Army Group, and therefore of all Allied ground forces at that time, the much-lauded British veteran of the North African desert campaigns had given General Omar Bradley's First US Army free reign to capture the Cotentin Peninsula. Montgomery then gave his full attention to the Anglo-Canadian Second Army, also under his command, to take Caen. Repeated operations to take Caen – Epsom, Charnwood and Goodwood – failed, coming at great loss of life. It was the lowest point in Montgomery's military career.

Operation Goodwood, July 1944. (Photo Sgt Christie)

On 15 July, Montgomery's XXX (British) Corps, under Lieutenant General Gerard Bucknall, renewed the Allies' efforts to clear the way to Caen from the north and west. Having recently joined the corps, the 59th (Staffordshire) Division took the left and the 50th the right in a fresh major assault. As part of the 59th's plan, elements of the Hallamshires would undertake a daylight frontal attack, with the objective of taking Barbee Farm and Vendes. With artillery support, D Company of 4/KOYLI took the right, and A Company under Major J. A. Nicholson, the left. C and D companies would remain where they were as battalion base, while B Company, under Major L.M. Lonsdale-Cooper, was in reserve.

The 4/KOYLI company was able to secure Barbee Farm, but strong German resistance halted A Company's advance 50yd short of Vendes church. B Company was then deployed to rendezvous with the 4/KOYLI at Barbee Farm, to launch a combined attack from that flank.

Yet again, the Germans put up a ferocious resistance, not only at Barbee Farm where the two companies were virtually surrounded, but in the larger picture, Hart Dyke received a message stating that both the 50th and 59th divisions' advance had ground to a halt for the day. Fearing that their positions at Barbee Farm would be overrun in the dark, the battalion commander made the difficult decision to withdraw B Company and the 4/KOYLI company. He left A Company in the position at Vendes.

Hart Dyke drew on all available fire power to execute the safe retirement of the two companies up the slope away from the farm. For half an hour, a sustained box barrage covered the withdrawal: all available mortars from the Hallamshires and 4/KOYLI, two machine-gun platoons from 2nd Battalion, Kensington Regiment (Princess Louise's), the Divisional Machine Gun Regiment, and two regiments of the Divisional Artillery. Both companies, including their casualties, withdrew safely.

The Hallamshires were then replaced by the Lincolnshire Regiment before moving to the rest area at Duchy St Marguerite for a week. They had been on the front line for thirty-three days, during which time the battalion had suffered 33 officers and 460 other ranks killed or wounded. Immediate awards were made to Lieutenant Colonel Hart Dyke, the Distinguished Service Order (DSO), and Captain P. G. Griffiths RAMC, the Military Cross.

On 23 July, the 49th Division was transferred to I Corps on the extreme left of the Allied front to the east and south-east of Caen. Commanded by Lieutenant General John Crocker, a week later, the corps came under the Canadian First Army, commanded by Lieutenant General Harry Crerar.

Commencing the first day of its advance from Poussy-la-Campagne, the men from Sheffield struck out to the north-east, occupying Billy then Airan. The next morning, they reached Les Pédouzes unopposed and threatening the German rear. The following day, Méry-Corbon was cleared three miles to the east, before the battalion, its carrier platoon blazing the way, stopped for the night at Le Lion d'Or. A mile to the east, the retreating Germans had destroyed the road bridge, so the following morning, the men crossed the river in boats, while battalion transport had to travel some distance into another brigade sector to cross on a Bailey bridge.

On 26 August, the battalion reached the south bank of the River Seine at the village of Vieuxport. All along the sector, Germans were fighting a rear-guard action as they employed anything that could float, including sixty ferries, to cross to the north bank. The main bottleneck was at the major bridge crossing, the Pont de Brotonne, at Port Caudebac. German resistance was so strong that the 146th Infantry Brigade was unable to get near the bridge, and the bulk of the German infantry was able to cross. However, the Hallamshires were able to take fifty-two Germans prisoner.

Officially, this marked the end of the Battle of Normandy. The defeated German army had jettisoned almost all their equipment so that the men could get away; horses, vehicles and stores cluttered the bridge approaches.

Since D-Day, the 21st Army Group had sustained heavy casualties, a fact that manifested itself in the disbandment of the 59th Division to replenish the strengths of other divisions. The Hallamshires absorbed a whole company of the disbanded 11th Battalion, the South Staffordshire Regiment, complete with its own commander, Major Grey.

In the first week of September, British armour entered Antwerp at the head of the Second British Army. The First Canadian Army was tasked with taking the Channel ports.

Crossing the Seine, August 1944 (Photo Sgt Laing)

Comprising the 49th and 51st divisions, I Corps was allocated the liberation of Le Havre. At Vieuxport, Hart Dyke and C Company crossed the Seine in a miscellany of damaged boats that they had found on the south bank. The rest of the battalion and all its equipment and stores crossed at Rouen.

It quickly became clear that the German garrison was going to fight it out. A decision was then taken to launch a full-scale attack by the whole of I Corps, initiated on 10 September by an air, sea and ground bombardment to soften up German defences.

The 49th Division conducted the frontal assault, while the 51st Division circled round to the north-east of the port. The next day, the Hallamshires and the Lincolns secured the town, with B and D companies reaching the edges of the docks. As the 51st Division penetrated the town to the north and the 49th the east, resistance in Le Havre ended. All that now remained was to secure the docks and to prevent the defeated German army from demolishing harbour installation to render the facility unusable.

This task became the sole responsibility of the Hallamshires. C Company was the first to advance, but as they crossed the Canal du Havre à Tancarville into the docks, there was a series of massive explosions, resulting in large chunks of concrete and steel from the lock gates crashing down among the troops. B and D companies followed, and after a few hours, only the South Mole offered any residual resistance by the Germans. The mole was a mile-long narrow strip of land on which the Germans had constructed large pill-boxes. At nightfall, Hart Dyke led D Company on to the mole, where they discovered that most of the pill-boxes had already been evacuated. By 10 pm, the mole was secured and more than eighty Germans taken prisoner.

In no small measure, the Hallamshires had played a leading role in the capture of Le Havre which had taken I Corps only two days to achieve. Of great significance is the fact that the battalion prevented the Germans from inflicting major damage to the docks.

On 19 September, the Hallamshires marched away from Le Havre, arriving three days later at Nijlen, fourteen miles south-east of Antwerp, with every one of its 105 vehicles in serviceable order.

Following the disastrous Allied airborne assault on Arnhem, the clearance of Antwerp gained importance as an alternative route to access the German industrial heartland of the Ruhr. On the 24th, the 146th Infantry Brigade would skirt Antwerp and head north-east for ten miles to cross the Antwerp–Turnhout Canal just before Rijkevorsel. From there, they would be transported east to Merksplas.

C and D companies' advance on the main route, however, stalled at an immense fortified German stronghold between the two towns. A former workhouse, the Depot de Mendicite, occupied a square-mile site to the north of the road. Dykes lined with high earthen embankments secured the position on three sides, in front of which the terrain was flat and open for a distance of 300yd.

On the morning of the 29th, while B and D companies protected the 147th Infantry Brigade's northern flank, C Company attacked the north-western boundary of the depot. At first light, the brigade's attack on the south and west of the depot encountered savage enemy resistance. Meanwhile C Company's leading platoon,

ON THE RHINE

Results have followed rapidly from the landing of the Airborne Army amid the waterways of central Holland at the week-end. The Second British Army, under General Dempsey, has thrust its armour forward from the Belgian border to join up with the paratroops.

It has cut through Holland as far as the outskirts of Nijmegen, an advance of 50 miles in 48 hours, crossing the Maas on the way, and reaching the Rhine just west of the German frontier where it goes under the Dutch name of Waal. To attain complete success it is necessary to cross the waterway and take Arnhem, on the north bank of the Lek, 10 miles ahead, which would mean that the line of the Rhine as well as the Siegfried Line had been turned.

That would bring about great strategic possibilities. The way would be open for a sweep into the north German plain, and there would be no serious obstacle to an advance in the direction of Berlin.

The Allied wedge is long and narrow. Field-Marshal Montgomery's first concern must be to widen it and strengthen it against flank attacks. This process is now being carried out. When our positions have been made secure the next stage will be not only to deepen the wedge, by driving it in still further, but to fan out, particularly to the west, with the object of encircling the German forces, reckoned at anything from 70,000 to 100,000, who are defending western Holland north of Antwerp.

These forces are being frontally attacked by the Canadians, so as to pin them down, and prevent them from disengaging. Naturally, the Allied Command are not giving any definite information about the positions our troops have reached, because that would assist the enemy in his counter-measures.

The Scotsman, Thursday, 21 September 1944

commanded by Lieutenant Judge, had reached the perimeter of their objective, but they were also held up by heavy enemy fire, in which Judge was wounded. The whole brigade attack ground to a halt and could move no further in support of the division's advance. It was at this stage that C Company's fortunes were turned around from an unlikely quarter.

One Corporal John William Harper assumed command of the platoon from the wounded Judge and, by his extremely courageous and sacrificial actions, allowed C Company to push on with their advance. A Company also took full advantage of the turn of events, striking at the northern defences of the depot with a troop of tanks in support. This also allowed elements of the Leicestershire Regiment to fight their way into some of the depot buildings.

Harper, a 28-year-old peat cutter from Doncaster, dashed across the 300yd open field of fire with his platoon, successfully scaled the wall, killed and captured the German soldiers, and secured his foothold.

After taking his prisoners back over the wall, and while still drawing mortar and Spandau machine-gun fire, Harper clambered back over the wall, by himself, to see if his platoon could ford the dyke, but it was too deep. Returning back over the wall to his men, he received a message instructing him to come up with a way to get his platoon over to the enemy side of the dyke. Undaunted, the dapper NCO went back over the wall for the third time, where he found unoccupied enemy weapons' dugouts, which he believed would provide safe positions for his platoon. Harper again cleared the wall to fetch his platoon, bringing them

The look of defeat on the face of a German soldier, Belgium, 1944. (Photo Bundesarchiv)

safely into the German dugouts. He lost only one man. Harper now set out, again on his own, to find a suitable point for his platoon to cross the dyke. Running along the dyke to his right, he found the rest of the battalion who had found a suitable place for the troops to ford. Harper's luck eventually ran out: he took a bullet and died on the bank of the dyke. (The full citation for the posthumous award of the Victoria Cross to Corporal Harper appears in Chapter 7.)

In spite of a strong German presence still in the depot, the Polish Armoured Division was now able to plough through it to take Merksplas. The Hallamshires followed, becoming the first unit in the 49th Division to reach the Netherlands. The towns of Weedle and Poppel were taken with little resistance, but on the left flank, B Company came up against strong resistance at Aerle. Platoon commander Lieutenant Wollerton would receive the Military Cross for his bravery in rescuing his wounded men.

No sooner had the Hallamshires consolidated their position at Aerle, when B and C companies, armed with mortars and anti-tank guns, were ordered one and a half miles north to the border village of Nieuwkerk to relieve the Divisional Reconnaissance Regiment which had become pinned down by a concentration of Germans in the area. With bolstered strengths in south-west Holland, the Germans had launched a counter-offensive. Along this front, Major Halford, who was in command of the two companies, was able to disperse a build-up of the enemy in front of Aerle. At the same time, however, a heavy contingent of German infantry and tanks moved against Nieuwkerk.

Infantry of the York and Lancaster Regiment in Fontenay-le-Pesnel, Normandy, June 1944. (Photo IWM)

A B Company platoon guarding the bridge was overrun, and tanks started to appear. At this new threat, Sergeant W. Newton and an anti-tank gun crew manoeuvred their gun into position to take on the tanks. Newton, now the only one of the crew not wounded, placed three well-directed shots at the leading tank, disabling it. British tanks now joined the fray, driving the enemy attack back and re-establishing a position on the bridge. Eleven members of the Hallamshires lost their lives in this fighting on 25 September, and are interred in the Leopoldsburg War Cemetery in Belgium.

Over the next two months, the Hallamshires continued to play a key role in the south-western Holland/northern Belgium campaign to clear Antwerp and re-open the port to the Allies. By mid-October, the Canadian First Army was reinforced by the arrival of the 52nd (Lowland) and the 104th US (Timber Wolf) Infantry divisions. From Wuustwezel in Belgium, on 20 October the 49th Division crossed into Holland and moved on Roosendaal. As the Germans withdrew, the 49th spent the night in Roosendaal, where commanders finalized arrangements for the eleven-mile thrust directly north to Willemstad on the Rhine estuary. Following a night march, B Company surprised the Germans in the village of Fijnaart, seven miles from Roosendaal.

At this stage of the campaign, the Hallamshires' strength had been significantly reduced to three companies and two platoons, including former anti-aircraft crews who had never seen action in an infantry role.

Hallamshires with liberated civilians, Ellecom, the Netherlands, April 1945. (Photo IWM)

Early in the morning of 6 November, A and C companies leapfrogged B Company's position at Fijnaart, with Oudemolen and Zwingelspaan, two miles to the north and northeast, as their respective objectives. A network of dykes restricted movement to the roads, which therefore necessitated getting in close to the objective under cover of darkness, followed by a rapid assault at first light. C Company took Zwingelspaan with relative ease, but to the west, A Company encountered a totally different situation.

Alert German sentries had detected the approach of the British troops on the road, and as it became light, Major Nicholson and his men came under heavy machine-gun fire. The men took to the dykes, pushing forward and firing their Bren guns at shoulder height. As Nicholson secured the eastern part of the village, the engagement developed into a street-by-street fight for possession. On the western side of the village, the two platoons of the former anti-aircraft crewmembers performed admirably, pushing their way towards A Company. However, heavy German machine-gun fire halted their advance. Across the village, Nicholson's situation had deteriorated. The Germans were counter-attacking with renewed vigour, while the British troops were almost out of ammunition. Nicholson and the two platoons to his west were immediately ordered to retire 300yd to allow support artillery to shell the village. This had the desired effect and A Company secured a now-deserted village. With the Hallamshires having established an east–west line, the Lincolnshire Regiment had a clear run to the Rhine. The battalion suffered forty-five casualties, including eight dead. The Hallamshires were then pulled back to Roosendaal for a welcome period of rest. The Channel ports from Le Havre, where the operation had commenced in September, to Antwerp, were now firmly in Allied hands – the men from Sheffield had led from the front.

Early in December, the battalion was assigned to what was known as the Nijmegen Island, a tract of farmland and villages between the Waal and Rhine rivers, which is about seven miles at its widest point. For the men, it was a tour of duty that lasted until March 1945, a lengthy period in which they dubbed themselves the 'Nijmegen Home Guard'. Periodically, to give the companies a break from the monotonous – but not always quiet – stint, the whole of B Echelon was also drafted in to do their bit.

The 'island' was of significant strategic importance to the Allies' North-West Europe campaign and the imminent Battle of the Rhineland, the stepping-stone into Nazi Germany. The principal idea was for the protection of the rear of the First Canadian Army in preparation of the offensive. However, the German counter-offensive in the Ardennes – the so-called Battle of the Bulge – meant the Rhineland operation was put off until the spring. The battalion would also protect the Arnhem–Nijmegen rail line, a key supply route to the front. Up to Christmas, when the battalion moved to Nijmegen for a period of rest, eighty-nine offensive patrols were conducted to capture a German prisoner for army headquarters. All attempts were unsuccessful. Elements from the disbanded, under-strength 50th Division now bolstered the Allied position on the island. Included was a

---

FLOODS INVADE NIJMEGEN-ARNHEM ISLAND

British guns are shelling the fortress town of Venlo, across the muddy waters of the Maas, but the Venlo operation is finished for the time being.

The flood waters of the Rhine area are spreading over the 'island' between Nijmegen and Arnhem, but the Allied bridgehead at Nijmegen is still secure.

The Germans have made no attempt to follow up Monday's attack on positions north of Nijmegen. Their intentions are not clear. Field-Marshal Montgomery's spokesman said, 'It's all rather queer. The attack was pointless.'

Almost all British forces have been withdrawn from the Nijmegen-Arnhem 'island', the German News Agency claimed. The rising water has made the fortifications practically useless, and the British are endeavouring to save their tanks and heavy batteries while the going is good. Apart from the Arnhem-Nijmegen highway, they have only the railway embankment, and both are being violently shelled day and night.

Dundee Courier, Wednesday, 6 December 1944

whole company of East Yorkshires, who were absorbed into the Hallamshires and retitled D Company. At the beginning of February, the 146th Infantry Brigade moved back on to the island, where the Hallamshires took over defence duties in the villages of Andelst and Zetten to the extreme west.

The previous month, a German counter-attack carried out in deep snow had been repelled. The snow had now melted, leaving large swathes of the countryside flooded. Platoons from the two companies in Zetten could only hold buildings unaffected by the floods. On the northern outskirts of the village, the Rijn Wettering could not be distinguished. Two miles to the south, the balance of the battalion and a troop of tanks held Andelst. Water separated the battalion from other units, making supply logistics problematic. Forward companies had to be replenished by amphibious vehicles, such as the six-wheeled American-made DUKW and M9 Weasel.

On 10 February, patrols waded out to the partly submerged hamlet of Hemmen, where, finding the place deserted, a patrol was left permanently. Proceeding north towards Indoornik, the other side of the Rijn Wettering, patrols quickly discovered that the Germans were firmly ensconced in the village, forcing them to fall back on Hemmen.

British troops shelter behind a disabled German PzKpfw III tank, Oosterhout, near Nijmegen, September 1944. (Photo Sgt Carpenter)

Just before first light every day, two pairs of battalion snipers would go out to find static positions from where they would spend the whole monitoring enemy movements. Lying still in the bitter cold was a task only for a dedicated few.

Private Metcalfe was one such soldier. One day, in a locality north of the Rijn Wettering, Metcalfe found himself surrounded by a German patrol oblivious to his immediate presence. Somehow, he was able to distract the German patrol long enough to sprint away and swim back across the Rijn Wettering. His waders, firmly lodged in cloying mud, remained behind. Metcalfe was subsequently decorated by the Dutch government.

With the commencement of the Battle of the Rhineland in mid-February, the 49th Division was ordered to substantially escalate its level of patrolling on the island to the extent that the Germans might be convinced that an Allied attack was looming. A platoon under Lieutenant Mitchinson was positioned at De Hooven Farm, where a three-storey farmhouse offered commanding views of the German stronghold at Randwijk, only 1,000yd to the west. However, the farm was a small islet in 6ft-deep flood water, and could only be reached by assault boat.

Soon, the whole of Hallamshires' B Company was north of the Rijn Wettering waterway. By stealth and operating at night, a platoon successfully landed on the southern outskirts of German-held Indoornik. On 20 February, another assault boat, ferrying half a B Company platoon to Talitha Kumi (where the main road crosses the Rijn Wettering), detonated a submerged mine, killing or drowning eight of the occupants and injuring two. Of the fatalities, all of them privates, five are interred in the Arnhem Oosterbeek War Cemetery, and three in the Jonkerbos War Cemetery in Nijmegen.

On the night of the 21st, Sergeant Joseph Newman and his platoon relieved Mitchinson at De Hooven Farm., but it was not an auspicious start. Rowing for five hours against a very strong current, Newman arrived at 11 pm, his boat loaded to the gunwales with supplies and wire to secure the farmhouse against a possible German attack. The three other boats with the rest of the platoon lost their way in the dark and only arrived at De Hooven the following morning at one o'clock.

At 2 am, the German garrison at Randwijk opened up on the De Hooven area with artillery and machine guns. An hour later, Hart Dyke retaliated with his own weapons and artillery, and for thirty minutes he fired on known German locations. At 3.40 am, a radio signal was received from Newman stating that the battalion's fire had been a success. That would be the last anyone would hear from the 37-year-old NCO.

In spite of the danger and fatigue, Lieutenant Mitchinson took a patrol out by boat to check on Newman and his platoon. What the officer found stunned not only him but the whole of the Hallamshire battalion. The farm building had been totally razed, and there was no sign of Newman and his men.

Only at the cessation of hostilities and the liberation of British prisoners of war, did the events of the 22nd come to light. Repatriated POWs reported that boats of German had silently closed in on De Hooven, where they raked the farmhouse with bazooka and sub-machine-gun fire. The Hallamshires inside did not stand a chance. Sergeant Newman was killed and Sergeant Potter and eight others severely wounded. The Germans then broke into the house, and took the whole platoon prisoner. It was a dark day for B Company and the battalion as a whole. B Company was immediately withdrawn from north of the Rijn Wettering.

At the end of February, Hart Dyke was transferred to Burma on promotion to brigadier, and on 11 March, Michael Charles Kirkpatrick Halford assumed command of the battalion with the rank of acting lieutenant colonel.

After four grim months, the Hallamshires returned to an aggressive role as the 49th Division prepared for the offensive against Arnhem. On 2 April, after 4/KOYLI and the Lincolns had established a bridgehead over the Rijn Wettering, D Company, under Major C. A. Mackillop attacked the front in troop carriers with anti-landmine flails in support. Major Woodward's D Company followed, their objective to clear the south bank of the Neder Rijn (Lower Rhine) in the direction of Arnhem.

D Company swept down the road, fighting and clearing the route all the way to the western outskirts of Kronenburg, three miles south of Arnhem, where enemy resistance forced a temporary halt. By now the flails had become unserviceable, themselves victims of mines and mud, but this did not deter D Company. Unsupported, they pushed the enemy back. Captain Robinson, Lieutenant Morris and six other ranks were wounded in

Anti-aircraft gun protecting a Bailey bridge at Arnhem. (Photo Sgt Hewitt)

the drive. Major Lonsdale-Cooper's C Company then sped through their sister company to take Elden. That night, the remaining German rear guard withdrew north across the Neder Rijn into Arnhem. Grasping the initiative, Lieutenant Edgson gathered a party and crossed the river, engaging the retreating enemy's rear. In so doing, the Hallamshires not only set a record by being the first troops of the 46th Division to cross the Seine, the Netherlands border and the Rhine, but proved their status as one of the finest battalions in the North-West Europe theatre.

On 5 April, B Squadron of the Divisional Reconnaissance Regiment relieved the Hallamshires. The battalion retired to Oosterhout, six miles south of Kronenburg, in readiness for a major assault on the city and the high ground beyond.

On the 12th, a sustained aerial attack by Hawker Typhoon fighter-bombers and an accompanying artillery bombardment heralded the commencement of the 46th Division's move on Arnhem. The 56th Infantry Brigade then established a secure bridgehead on the north bank of the Neder Rijn. The following day, Friday, the 13th, the Lincolns led the 146th Infantry Brigade across the river. The objective of the brigade was to take the eastern half of Arnhem, which would allow the Hallamshires to pass through to take the heights overlooking the city.

In the afternoon, the battalion boarded LVT-4 (landing vehicle tracked) Buffalo IVs at their concentration area, and arrived in the assembly area on the north bank at 4.30 pm. The Lincolns, however, met stiff enemy resistance, retarding the whole east Arnhem operation. Instead of striking north to their objective in daylight, it was 7.30 pm when the Hallamshires eventually got under way.

Halford had tasked his men to attack with one company at a time. In each case, this would be preceded by a concentrated artillery bombardment and a 'mattress'. The latter was the Land Mattress, a 30- or 60-tube rocket launching system that fired 5ft 10in-long rockets weighing 67lb each. The next company would then leapfrog the first company, and so on.

A dense forest covered the south-facing slopes of the heights above Arnhem, the battalion's objective. Over the ridge there were army barracks, and beyond that, a road junction. At 7.30 pm, Major Grey led B Company half way up the tree-covered slope and halted. C Company, commanded by Major Lonsdale-Cooper followed, pushing through B Company, but finding the going extremely difficult in the dark. By 10 pm, Lonsdale-Cooper attained his objective by taking the barracks. Major Mackillop and his D Company came next, reaching a road junction at 11 pm. At first light, A Company, under Major Woodward, passed through D Company and fought their way to the final battalion objective: the road junction to the north of the barracks. In the fighting, Lieutenant Ronald Davies was killed. The previous day, 13 April, privates E. C. Norman and T. Rayner also lost their lives. All three Hallamshire men are also buried in the Arnhem Oosterbeek War Cemetery.

Arnhem would be the battalion's combat swansong. On 7 May, the Hallamshires joined a motorized column for a liberation parade through Utrecht, a fitting end to their eleven-month expedition since Normandy. The battalion remained in Germany as part of the British occupying forces until 1946, when it returned home.

6pdr anti-tank gun of the 4th Hallamshires guarding the road to Willemstad, the Netherlands, November 1944. (Photo Sgt Wilkes)

WE ARE MAKING SURE OF ARNHEM

YORK AND LANCS MEN OVER RHINE: COAST THRUST

British troops are again at the gates of Arnhem, and this time there will be no failure. Arnhem's doom is sealed. British patrols – men of the 49th (West Riding) Division – crossed the river last night and the night before. They were the first British to set foot on the north bank of the Lower Rhine [Neder Rijn] since the epic of the First Airborne Division last September.

An officer and nine men of the York and Lancaster Regiment [Hallamshires] went over the river in an assault boat and inland. Every man returned.

Men of the 49th Division opposite Arnhem are nearer to the Zuider Zee than any other troops of the [First] Canadian Army of liberation. From Arnhem to the coast is less than twenty-three miles.

The iron ring is indeed closing on Holland.

Liverpool Daily Post, Friday, 6 April 1945

4. THEY SERVED

Field Marshal Herbert Charles Onslow Plumer, 1st Viscount Plumer, GCB, GCMG, GCVO, GBE

Born on 13 March 1857 in Kensington, London, Plumer is without question Sheffield's most famous and esteemed soldier, and, accorded the burial status of a hero in Westminster Abbey, also one of Britain's most distinguished.

Educated at Eton, Plumer entered Sandhurst, from which he received a commission in September 1876 into the 65th Regiment of Foot, thereby commencing a life-long association with Sheffield. At the end of that year, Plumer undertook his first overseas tour of duty when he joined his regiment in Lucknow, India, where he assumed the position of adjutant.

Following the Cardwell reforms that saw the 65th merge with the 84th to form the 1st Battalion, the York and Lancaster Regiment, Plumer was promoted to captain in May 1882. The young officer's next deployment was to the Sudan, where the battalion arrived in February 1884 as part of the Nile Expedition, a British task force to relieve Major General Charles Gordon at Khartoum. On 29 February 1884, Plumer had his first taste of battle at El Teb. However, the battle at Tamai the following month, in which 2,000 Sudanese were slaughtered, had a profound and lasting effect on Plumer. Not only was it his twenty-seventh birthday, but the loss of thirty-two of his men killed and twenty-two wounded, compelled him to mention the 'awful battle of Thursday' to his fiancée: 'One longed to see active service, but I have seen enough to last me some time'. As a field marshal, Plumer would have a deep respect for the lives of the men he committed to war.

Back in England in July, Plumer married Annie Constance.

Lieutenant General Herbert Plumer, 1917.

He enrolled at the Staff College, Camberley, passing out in 1887, before taking up an appointment as deputy-assistant adjutant general in Jersey in 7 May 1890. During this three-year tour of duty, Plumer wrote his first of only two articles: 'The Military Resources of the Island of Jersey'.

He was promoted to major in 22 January 1893 and posted to the 2nd Battalion, the York and Lancaster Regiment in South Africa, a posting that British officers regarded, at the time, as a backwater.

Early in 1895, he met the diamond magnate, Cecil John Rhodes, and the colonialist's close associate and confidant, the impetuous Dr Leander Starr Jameson. In the spring, Plumer was back in England to spend time with his family. In spite of numerous representations to the War Office for a different posting, in November the disillusioned Plumer was back in South Africa, now determined to resign from the army.

He was then appointed acting military secretary to the General Officer Commanding, Cape Colony in December 1895. His fate to remain in the sub-continent had been sealed, which was, for the 38-year-old, a fortuitous turning point in his military career. Rumours of an impending conflict with the two South African Boer republics – Transvaal and Orange Free State – would unwittingly draw Plumer into both war and prominence.

Just before the New Year, Jameson, to the bewilderment of the local British administration in South Africa and London, invaded the Transvaal Republic with a nondescript, ragtag mounted force of 600 to 'liberate' Johannesburg – the infamous fiasco that was the Jameson Raid. The outcome, on 2 January 1896, was an unmitigated disaster, causing Britain unimaginable embarrassment.

Within days, Plumer was sent to Mafeking and Bulawayo, in anticipation of a Transvaal backlash. However, there was no immediate concern, and Plumer returned to the Cape in March. He had barely arrived when he was sent to Matabeleland where the amaNdebele nation had come out in rebellion. Meeting up with fellow York and Lancaster officer, Major Frederick Kershaw, at Mafeking, Plumer raised the 750-strong Matabeleland Relief Force (MRF). The first contingent left for Matabeleland on 12 April.

At the end of June, Plumer marched on the Matopos Hills, the granite-bouldered stronghold and spiritual home of the amaNdebele.

Lieutenant Colonel Plumer in Matabeleland, August 1896.

Plumer's campaign was a success, and in November, he was back in Cape Town, before making it back to England for Christmas, where, he had become a household name. Rhodesian administrator and future Governor General of Canada, Earl Grey had this to say:

> The fact that Colonel Plumer was able to raise, horse and equip at Mafeking a force of over 700 men and fight two successful battles against the Matabele, after marching 600 miles within forty-one days of the receipt of the first order given to raise the force, is, if not a unique, at any rate a very remarkable achievement.
>
> And not less remarkable than this achievement was the admirable discipline and bearing of the force thus hurriedly collected throughout the whole of their service in Matabeleland.

Plumer spent the first two months of 1897 writing his only book, *An Irregular Corps in Matabeleland.*

In August 1899, Plumer was back in Bulawayo, this time to raise two local mounted regiments to protect the border with the north-west Transvaal from Boer invasion at the start of the Anglo-Boer War – one regiment from Rhodesia and one from Bechuanaland. In the early months, Plumer, after several skirmishes, successfully prevented any meaningful Boer insurgencies across the Limpopo River into Rhodesia through his deployment of squadrons of the Rhodesia Regiment to the various drifts through the river.

Republican gun at Mafeking. (Photo Hennie Heymans)

Plumer then headed south through Bechuanaland, along the rail line to the besieged Mafeking. At the end of March 1900, having overcome strong Boer resistance at Crocodile Pools, Plumer reached Mafeking, but to his chagrin, the promised relief column from the south had not arrived. The outcome, had it not been for Plumer's leadership attributes, would have been disastrous. Seeing Plumer approaching with 350 men, a far superior enemy force surrounded Plumer's column. Although sustaining wounds to his arm and wrist, he was able to fight a rear-guard action to escape back to Gaberones (now Gaborone). The contingent's casualties amounted to forty-nine killed and wounded, in addition to the loss of seventy-five horses. The magnanimous Plumer gave up his horse to a wounded soldier and, leading his mount, walked back through the hot, arid bush to the Bechuanaland capital.

MAFEKING SIEGE

BADEN-POWELL'S MESSAGE

Colonel Baden-Powell has sent the following message to Lord Roberts:

'After two hundred days' siege, I desire to bring to your lordship's notice the exceptionally good spirits and loyalty that pervade all classes of the garrison. The patience of everyone in Mafeking in making the best of things under the long strain of anxiety, hardships, and privation is beyond all praise, and is a revelation to me.

'The men, half of whom are unaccustomed to the use of arms, have adapted themselves to their duties with the greatest zeal, readiness, and pluck, and the devotion of the women is remarkable.

'With such a spirit our organisation runs like clockwork and I have every hope it will pull us successfully through.

'Since the abortive attempt on the 25th inst. to attack the south-western forts, the enemy has been comparatively quiet.

'The citizens are preparing to celebrate the two hundredth day of the siege by horse dinners.

'It is suggested here that the funds which we see from the Cape newspapers are to be employed in festivities on the relief of Mafeking should be devoted to defraying the cost of a trip to the sea of all the women and children who have gone through the siege.'

(Reuter's Telegram)

Mafeking, April 24th.

The town and garrison have made up their minds to hold out at all costs.

The first issue of horse sausage took place yesterday.

Western Daily Press, Wednesday, 9 May 1900

On 14 May, his regiment reinforced, and with the fresh arrival through Rhodesia of colonial troops from Australia and New Zealand, Plumer again set off to Mafeking. Colonel Mahon was approaching from the south with the other relief column. The Boers, however, put up a bitter fight, and it was only just before first light on the 17th that the Mafeking siege finally ended. Again, however, Plumer's casualties were high.

For Plumer there would be no break. Still with remnants of his Rhodesian column, Plumer participated in the seemingly endless British chase after elusive Boer generals, de la Rey, de Wet and Botha. In March 1902, his column was disbanded, Acting Brigadier General Plumer returned to England to a hero's welcome. On 12 May, he attended an investiture where King Edward VII appointed him a Companion of the Order of the Bath.

Later that year, Plumer was promoted to major general; at 45, one of the youngest in the British army. In December 1903, he was appointed General Officer Commanding (GOC) both 10th Division and Eastern District. Following a transfer to Ireland as GOC 5th Division, Plumer was promoted to the rank of lieutenant general in November 1908, which also saw him returning to London. In November 1911, he was appointed GOC Northern Command, then encompassing the counties of Northumberland, Cumberland, Westmoreland, Durham, Lancashire, Yorkshire and the Isle of Man.

With the outbreak of hostilities in Europe in August 1914, the British Expeditionary Force (BEF), comprising I and II corps, under the command of Sir John French, arrived in France. Lieutenant General Sir James Moncrieff Grierson, commander of II Corps, died of a heart attack soon after arriving in France. French immediately wired newly appointed Secretary of State for War Lord Kitchener, writing, 'I recommend that Lieutenant-General Plumer may be appointed to fill vacancy caused by unfortunate death of General Grierson'. French's long-standing friend, Lieutenant General Sir Ian Hamilton also put in a bid, but Kitchener appointed the commander at Aldershot, Lieutenant General Sir Horace Smith-Dorrien. French appealed:

> I had already wired asking you to appoint *Plumer* in his place, when your wire reached here and also that of Ian Hamilton forwarded – as I understand – by you.
>
> I very much hope that you will send me Plumer – Hamilton is too senior to command an Army Corps and is already engaged on an important command at home. *Plumer*. Do as I ask you in this matter. I needn't assure you there was no 'pressure' of any kind.

Kitchener would not budge, however, and Plumer was given command of V Corps. After the Second Battle of Ypres of April 1915, in May, Plumer succeeded Smith-Dorrien as commander of the Second Army and promoted to full general in June.

In June 1917, Plumer scored an overwhelming tactical victory against the Germans at the Battle of Messines in Flanders, Belgium. Even the 25,000 British, Australian, New Zealand and Canadian casualties failed to dampen the satisfaction of BEF commander, Field Marshal Douglas Haig:

George V, centre, with British army commanders at Buckingham Palace. Plumer is third from the left. (Photo IWM)

> The complete success of the attack made yesterday by the Second Army under the command of General Sir Plumer is an earnest of the eventual victory of the Allied cause ... I desire to place on record here my deep appreciation of the splendid work done, above and below ground as well as in the air, by all Army, Services, and Departments, and by the Commanders and Staffs by whom, under Sir Herbert Plumer's orders, all means at our disposal were combined, both in preparation and execution, with a skill, devotion and bravery beyond all praise.

Plumer went on to win further victories at the battles of the Menin Road Ridge and Polygon Wood in September 1917, and of Broodseinde in October.

In November, a stunned and hugely disappointed Plumer was given command of the BEF on the Italian Front. In a letter to his wife, he wrote, 'I have just received a great shock. I have been ordered to go to Italy to assume command of the British Forces there. I am very sick about it and do not want to go in the least.' Turing down the position of Chief of the Imperial General Staff, to replace Field Marshal Sir William Robert Robertson, Plumer resumed his command of the Second Army during the closing stages of the war.

Field Marshal Plumer's full dress uniform (see colour plates). (Photo Gerry van Tonder)

Following the Armistice, in December 1918 Plumer was appointed General Officer Commanding-in-Chief, the British Army of the Rhine, before becoming Governor of Malta in May the following year.

On 31 July 1919, Plumer was promoted to field marshal and, later that year, created Baron Plumer of Messines and of Bilton. In October 1925, he was appointed High Commissioner of the British Mandate for Palestine, where he strongly defended the Balfour Declaration, while maintaining a firm hand over both Jewish and Arab nationalists.

Plumer was created Viscount Plumer on 3 June 1929, and on 16 July 1932, he passed away at his home in Knightsbridge, London. He was buried in Westminster Abbey.

Major Frederick Kershaw

Frederick Kershaw was born in 1860 in Edmonton, London, the son of Burroughs Dickie Kershaw ('gentleman') and Mary Ann Margaret.

Upon receiving his commission on 13 March 1880, the young subaltern was stationed at Ashton-under-Lyme with the 6th Royal Lancashire Militia. On 18 May 1881, Kershaw was promoted to the rank of lieutenant, and in July the following year, he was transferred from the 4th Battalion, the Manchester Regiment, to the York and Lancaster Regiment. On 8 July 1889, he was appointed adjutant, a position he held until his resignation from the post in November 1891. He had, by this time, risen to the rank of captain.

In distant southern Africa, the stabbing and shooting to death of a native policeman by amaNdebele warriors under induna Umbozo on the night of 20 March 1896, signalled the mass insurrection of the indigenous peoples of Matabeleland, as their dissatisfaction with the presence of the settlers and their arrogant native police erupted into an orgy of violence, which would witness the murder of 145 white men, women and children scattered throughout the remote countryside. In sporadic engagements with the amaNdebele over the following months, locally formed militia units, together with the later arrival of the Matabeleland Relief Force (MRF) under Lieutenant Colonel Herbert Plumer, would eventually force the rebels to put down their weapons and seek peace from Cecil Rhodes in their traditional and spiritual stronghold in the Matopos hills.

Plumer, a major with the 2nd Battalion, the York and Lancaster Regiment, had been given the local rank of lieutenant colonel and tasked by the High Commissioner in South Africa, Sir Hercules Robinson, to raise a relief force. Captain Frederick Kershaw, given the local rank of major, also of the 2nd Battalion, had arrived in Mafeking from Cape Town with Plumer in the April, together with a further 154 officers and other ranks of the battalion. Other officers included doctors R. Hutton and A. Rutt, captains C. H. Kekewich and F. M. Shadwell, and lieutenants J. S. Armstrong, M. Middleton and H. P. Thurnall.

Enrolment of a corps of 750 took place simultaneously in Kimberley and Mafeking, with Major Kershaw also responsible for assembling all the kit and equipment in Mafeking. The corps eventually numbered 850 active men, including some 400 from the Bechuanaland Border Police and the British South Africa Company Police. The balance was mainly made up of miners, engineers, farmers and clerks. Most were English-born colonials, with a significant contingent of Dutch Afrikanders. Pay would range from 7/6d a day for a trooper, to 15/- for a regular officer. Each man was issued with a Martini-Henry rifle and allocated 250 rounds of ammunition, with 50 rounds to be carried on his person at any one time. The corps deployed with 45 mule-drawn wagons and 1,150 mounts,

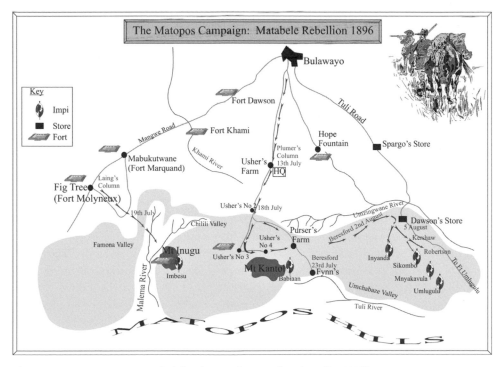

The Matopos campaign, Matabeleland, 1896. (Map Colonel Dudley Wall)

leaving Mafeking for Bulawayo in fourteen detachments over a two-week period in April 1896. Seven Maxim guns, purchased from Durban, were sent up later.

In addition to his position as Plumer's second-in-command, Kershaw was placed in command of C Squadron, made up of volunteers from Johannesburg. The squadron was made up of six officers, 145 men, 180 horses, 93 mules and seven wagons.

Elements of the MRF were soon engaged in action with the rebel impis at Gwaai, Umguza, Khami, and the mission station at Hope Fountain where a fort had been erected. On 2 June, the Salisbury Column, which included Cecil John Rhodes, having been met by Colonel Napier's column at the Shangani River Drift, arrived in Bulawayo. Major General Sir Frederick Carrington arrived on the same day to assume overall command of the troops. He was accompanied by his chief staff officer, Lieutenant Colonel Robert Baden-Powell.

At 10.30 pm on the night of 19 July, Plumer's MRF column, comprising 800 men, 300 'friendlies', two 2.5in. guns and three Maxims, set off in the moonlight towards the Chilili Valley in the Matopos. By this time, Lord Albert Grey, Cecil John Rhodes and his brother Frank had joined the expedition. (see the Matopos Campaign map in the colour plates section.)

On the morning of 5 August, Captain The Honourable J. Beresford (7th Hussars) took a force of 138 dismounted men in a westerly direction to gain a strategic ridge. Progress was slow and uncertain, but as they neared the summit, their right flank came under attack from 50yd. Lieutenant Hubert Hervey (MRF), with twenty men, tried to repel the enemy advance, but upon gaining the crest he fell, badly wounded. Battery Sergeant Major Alexander Ainslie (MMP) replaced him, but was immediately shot and killed. At this time, the rebels also started closing in from the front and the left, with the intention of overrunning the now tenuous position.

The two guns were immediately unloaded and brought into action, Lieutenant McCulloch opening fire with case shot to the front and right flank, and Lieutenant Fraser the left. Within the first few minutes, both were wounded, but they remained with their guns, desperately fending off the encircling amaNdebele.

As soon as the firing began, the friendlies carrying the Hotchkiss dropped their cargo and, in Plumer's own words, ran off behind some rocks 'in the most cowardly manner'. As a consequence, part of the gun could not be found, so this weapon could not be brought into action. Off to one side, Captain Llewellyn gallantly and singlehandedly worked his Maxim, even as his weapon and rocks around him were being hit by incoming gunfire. His assistant, 18-year-old Trooper Evelyn Holmes (MRF), was badly wounded and unable to assist Llewellyn, who now also had a face injury from rock splinters. Holmes would succumb to his wounds four days later.

Their line of communication and retreat cut off from the rear, Beresford and his party held out until 10 am, when the rebels retreated 500yd off.

When news eventually came through to Plumer informing him that Beresford could not advance without reinforcements, Plumer immediately ordered his whole force forward. With Baden-Powell and his scouts in front, the Colenbrander and Robertson Cape

Locally raised troops man a Maxim machine gun, Matabele Rebellion, 1896.

Boys marched out, followed by two Maxims and mounted troops. C, D and E squadrons, led by Major Kershaw, Captain Fraser and Captain Drury, respectively, galloped off to the left in support of the Cape Boys, while the MMP under Captain Nicholson, A Squadron, and two Maxims were sent to assist Beresford off to the right.

Upon reaching the base of the hills, the squadrons, led by Kershaw, dismounted and joined the Cape Boys in the assault. Sergeant Archibald Innes-Kerr (MRF) was shot and killed as the ascent commenced. The rebels' line started to yield, especially with the added pressure of heavy crossfire from Beresford's position.

The climb, however, was very difficult, the attackers having to climb over very large boulders. About halfway up and leading his men all the way, Major Frederick Kershaw was shot and killed. As the troops reached the summit, sergeants William Gibbs (MRF) and Oswald McCloskie (MRF) were both shot and killed.

By 2 pm, the rebels were in disorganized and rapid retreat. Plumer described the actions that day as the 'severest we had had'. One officer and four sergeants lay dead, and Lieutenant Hervey died of his wounds the following day. Estimates put the amaNdebele force at 3,000, of which 200 were accounted for. General Carrington and Cecil Rhodes arrived the next day, when a parade was held and the troops congratulated on a successful operation.

MATABELELAND

The Matabeleland and Mashonaland territories constitute the most promising for colonisation in the whole of South Africa. Compared with the country south of it, Matabeleland is like Canaan after the wilderness. Lying high, generally healthy, it is also very rich in minerals – gold, copper, and iron having, as it is known, been very extensively worked by the ancients with their rude appliances. Its numerous rivers are either running or have plenty of water in them at all times. The soil is rich and admirably adapted for corn; cattle thrive, and there is abundance of grass and wood.

White children can be reared in the country, which is a SINE QUA NON if it is to be successfully colonised by white men; and above all, it is sparsely populated.

The country dominated by the Matabele is nearly as large as Germany, while the territory actually occupied by them is very small, and would compare about as Bavaria does to the German Empire. Their kraals occupy the plateau forming the water-parting between the Zambezi and Crocodile [Limpopo] rivers. They are a Zulu military organisation, occupying a rich country which they have depopulated, and live under a despotism of the worst kind. Their fighting strength is probably not over 14,000 to 15,000 men. The history of the Matabele nation has been one of bloodshed since their exodus from Zululand under Mzilikazi about 1822.

Of their government little can be said, except that everything centres in the king. Their laws relate principally to witchcraft. There has been less raiding [against the Mashona] though this will never cease until their organisation is destroyed. King Lobengula, gross and savage as he undoubtedly is, is by no means so black as he is painted. He has to rule a turbulent people, who do not know the value of life. He is shrewd, possesses a wonderful memory, and has sufficient intuitive knowledge to despise many of the superstitions, of which, he is the chief exponent.

But the country has great possibilities, and the attitude of its natives towards the white settlers in the neighbourhood is a matter of universal interest.

Jarrow Express, Friday 20 October 1893

In his book on the campaign, *An Irregular Corps in Matabeleland*, Plumer wrote:

All did well in the assault, C Squadron of the M.R.F. being perhaps especially conspicuous. Major Kershaw's death was a severe loss to the force. In this and other actions he had shown himself a particularly able and gallant officer, and with his quiet, unassuming manner he had won the respect and affection of all ranks.

Poor Hervey died about 12 noon this day. He and Kershaw and the others who fell that day were all buried near our camp under a big tree. There is a fort [Umlugulu] there now, and the graves we know will be well looked after.

The hill in the Matopos, with a white cross indicating where Major Frederick Kershaw fell on 5 August 1896. The inset is of the memorial to those who died in the campaign. (Photo Alan Bryant)

Acting Captain Vivian Sumner Simpson MC

Vivian Sumner Simpson was born at Beech House in Sheffield on 5 February 1883, to solicitor George Joseph Simpson and his wife Gertrude. The youngest of nine children, he was educated at Wesley College, Sheffield, before joining his father's firm.

Upon completing his schooling, Simpson joined Sheffield Football Club, appearing for the club for the first time in the 1900–01 season. Affectionately known by all as 'Simmy', the all-round sportsman also excelled at cricket and golf.

Over the next seven years, Simpson scored thirty-eight goals in as many appearances, the most famous being a hat-trick when Sheffield thrashed Manchester United 6–0. He was also regarded as being largely responsible for Sheffield greatest moment: winning the 1904 Amateur Cup.

With the outbreak of the First World War, Simpson was one of the first to enlist with one of the new 'Pals' battalions, the 12th (Sheffield) Service Battalion, the York and Lancaster Regiment.

Commissioned with the rank of temporary second lieutenant on 27 January 1915, in July 1916, Simpson found himself with the 12th on the Western Front, participating in the monumental Somme offensive launched on 1 July. Simpson survived the horrors of the prolonged battle.

In May 1917, he was promoted to acting captain in the 12th. At this time, the battalion was in the Arras area, where the 31st Division had been brought forward to capitalize on the Canadian success at Vimy Ridge. After a brief period of 'rest' away from the front line, on 14 June, the battalion relieved the 14th at Gavrelle, but five

Captain Vivian Sumner Simpson MC, 12th (Sheffield) Battalion.

days later, their brigade was pulled back to rehearse for an imminent attack in the Gavrelle-Oppy sector. The battalion was tasked with taking and holding a section of the German line known as Cadorna Trench, a strategically important objective.

At 7 pm on 28 June, ladders were secured to the trench walls and bayonets quietly fixed. At 7.10 pm, British artillery opened up with a heavy bombardment of the German line, and at the same time, A, C and D companies of the 12th clambered out of their trenches into no man's land in three waves that were only 20yd apart from each other. The 12th did not sustain a single casualty and, taking numerous Germans prisoner, immediately set about revetting the erstwhile enemy trench – sandbags, wire, ammunition and supplies came flooding across no man's land.

In the action to capture Cadorna Trench, Simpson led his company from the front. His bravery would earn him the Military Cross:

The London Gazette, 14 September 1917

For conspicuous gallantry and devotion to duty during and after an attack upon enemy trenches. He was the first to reach the trench, and to be engaged in hand-to-hand fighting with the enemy. Later, he displayed the greatest ability and energy in organising his company for the work of protection and consolidation. His work has been consistently excellent on previous occasions.

On 16 July, while the battalion was at Vimy area, General Haig arrived to present Simpson with his Military Cross.

On 18 September, the battalion was allocated brigade support in Brown Trench. A Company was tasked with a raid on the German lines, so preparatory reconnaissance patrols into no man's land had to be conducted. As company commander, Simpson elected to lead a second patrol, during which he sustained a bullet wound to the arm. The disappointed officer was invalided home, where he was posted to Sunderland to train junior officers. Albeit that Simpson had a propensity for the task, he instead elected to return to his unit at the front.

Early in 1918, the decimated British units were re-organized. The 31st Division was disbanded, and the majority of the 12th Battalion was absorbed by the 13th.

It was at this time, on 13 April 1918, that Simpson was shot and killed by a sniper in the village of Outtersteene. The brave 33-year-old officer was buried in the Outtersteene Communal Cemetery Extension, Bailleul, France.

Captain Simpson's first grave on the Western Front.

5. THE UNITS

The York and Lancaster Regiment

General Order No. 41 of 1 May 1881, embodied significant changes in the structure of the British army under the new Secretary of State, Hugh Childers. It was thus on 1 July that year, that five hitherto independent regiments in Yorkshire and Lancashire were merged in pursuance of the so-called county regiment system into a single military formation. The York and Lancaster Regiment would comprise five battalions:

1st Battalion, the former 65th Foot
2nd Battalion, the former 84th Foot
3rd Battalion, the old militia
4th (Hallamshire) Battalion, the former Hallamshire Rifles
5th Battalion, the former 8th West Riding Volunteers

65th Regiment of Foot

The 65th was raised in 1756 as a second battalion of 12th (Suffolk) Regiment of Foot. Two years later, the regiment became an independent unit, commanded by Colonel Robert Armiger. The regiment first saw active service in the Caribbean and West Indies from 1759 to 1964, participating in the taking of Guadeloupe and Havana.

65th Regiment of Foot shako.
(Photo Gerry van Tonder)

The regiment went on to serve in the American War of Independence, participating in the Battle of Bunker Hill in June 1775. In 1782, the regiment was retitled the 65th (2nd Yorkshire, North Riding) Regiment of Foot. Over the next few years, the regiment was stationed at Gibraltar, Canada and Nova Scotia, before returning to the West Indies in 1794.

From a posting to South Africa in 1800, followed by Ceylon (1802) and Mauritius (1810), the 65th performed anti-pirate operations in the Persian Gulf until its return to Britain in 1822. This earned the regiment the unique battle honour 'Arabia'.

In May 1846, the regiment sailed for the Antipodes, seeing action in the New Zealand Wars against the Maoris.

EXTRACT OF A LETTER FROM LONDON, TO A FRIEND AT BOSTON:

Never did I feel myself so anxious about public affairs as at this moment. Our own interest is intimately connected with the perseverance of our American brethren in their opposition to the tyranny of our government.

Should they continue firm, it will be scarcely possible that they should not succeed.

I cannot help believing that this will be the last struggle which America will have with us. If they are now steady, and succeed, they will have no reason to fear any future attempts to enslave them. But if they now submit, they will be subdued for ever, and the only nursery of freemen now in the world will be lost. May Heaven avert such a calamity! I cannot indeed imagine a state of worse slavery than that in which the colonies would be, were they on this occasion to submit.

The present state of our parliament is such, that it is our own greatest calamity to be governed by it. How base would it be to wish the Americans involved in the same calamity!

The Scots Magazine, Wednesday, 1 March 1775

Returning home in 1866, the regiment was deployed to Ireland the following year to help quell the Fenian Uprising in 1867 (see Chapter 2). From 1871 to 1880, the 65th was again stationed in India.

The regiment's badge incorporates the Royal Tiger and the Union Rose, the latter a combination of the White Rose of the Duchy of York and the Red Rose of the Duchy of Lancaster. The ducal coronet above the emblems represents the old Duchy of Lancaster.

84th Regiment of Foot
Initially raised in York in November 1793 in response to fears over the potential ramifications of the revolution in France, the 84th served briefly in the Netherlands, before moving to South Africa and then India. To reflect the counties of origin of the two battalions that made up the regiment, in 1808 is was retitled the 84th (York and Lancaster) Regiment of Foot.

84th Regiment of Foot shako.
(Photo Gerry van Tonder)

In 1819, the two battalions amalgamated. Prior to this, the 1st served in Mauritius and India, while the 2nd saw action in the Netherlands and the Peninsular Wars.

The regiment went on perform convict transport escort duties to New South Wales and New Zealand, before a posting to the West Indies. They were then stationed in India for fourteen years from 1845, where they saw considerable action during the Indian Mutiny of 1857. Six members of the 84th were awarded the Victoria Cross for acts of gallantry during the siege and relief of Lucknow.

Militias

During the eighteenth- and nineteenth-century Anglo-French conflicts, and with many of the regular British regiments posted overseas, there was a growing concern that the country was vulnerable to invasion by the French. As a direct consequence, militias were raised throughout Britain. In July 1758, the Marquis of Rockingham invited men who might be interested in becoming militia officers to a meeting at Pontefract. This resulted in the formation of the 3rd West Yorkshire Militia, with Colonel Thornton as its first commanding officer.

One of Sheffield's town guns. (Photo Gerry van Tonder)

The Sheffield Loyal Independent Volunteers, raised in April 1794, was another such unit, commanded by Colonel R. A. Althorpe, and comprising about 490 men. Artillery pieces, the Town Guns, were subsequently made for the regiment. The 6-pdrs had 5ft-long barrels, and a range of between 350–2,000 yards.

The unit was mobilized in August 1795 when another newly raised regiment mutinied as they had not been paid. The Sheffield Volunteers were ordered to fire on the dissenters in Norfolk Street. The unit was disbanded in 1802.

The threat of invasion, however, did not materialize.

In the face of further perceived threats from the continent in the 1850s, county lord lieutenants were tasked with raising local volunteer units. Led by civilians, such rifle volunteer corps were raised in Sheffield, Rotherham, Barnsley and Doncaster.

The Hallamshires

Hallamshire is the name of the old Saxon manor surrounding Sheffield, so it was therefore an appropriate title for the voluntary infantry unit formed on 27 June 1859, the Hallamshire Rifles.

By December that year, the battalion had four companies on its strength, and was given the title the 2nd West Riding of Yorkshire (Hallamshire) Volunteer Rifle Corps.

In January 1861, the founding commanding officer, Major Wilson-Overend stood down, to be replaced by Lord Wharncliffe as lieutenant colonel of the unit.

The first uniform, selected and approved by the West Riding Lord Lieutenant, was described as:

Light grey with scarlet facings;
Austrian knot on cuff in black cord;
Trousers grey with black stripe. Narrow scarlet band down middle of stripe;
Grey forage cap with straight peak, black oak leaf band;
Black waist belt;
Officers and sergeants, crimson sash as infantry of the line;
Black sword belt;
Grey chaco, pattern as infantry of the line;
Buttons to be of green bronze bearing the Sheffield Corporate Arms, surrounded by the words 'Dieu est mon ecu'.

The men were issued with the British percussion service rifle, the .577cal. Lancaster.

The first regimental colours were presented in 1862 by Lady Mary Thompson on behalf of the Sheffield Mechanics' Institution. They were ultimately laid up in the Sheffield Parish Church in 1910. In January 1883, the battalion was retitled the 1st (Hallamshire) Volunteer Battalion of the York and Lancaster Regiment. Three years later they moved into their new headquarters at Hyde Park Barracks.

With the outbreak of the Anglo-Boer War in 1899, 275 members of the Hallamshires volunteered for active serve in South Africa.

With the introduction of the Territorial Army Scheme, in 1908, the battalion was retitled to the 4th (Hallamshire) Battalion, the York and Lancaster Regiment. At this time, Lieutenant Colonel George Ernest Branson VD, assumed command of the battalion, its strength now standing at 34 officers and 767 other ranks.

In the First World War, the first and second line battalions of the 4th lost 45 officers and 1,325 other ranks in action. During the conflict, the battalion earned a Victoria Cross – Acting Sergeant John Brunton Daykins (see Chapter 7) – 5 Distinguished Service Orders, 57 Military Crosses, 45 Distinguished Conduct Medals and 111 Military Medals.

In 1913, the Territorial Association for the Hallamshires purchased Endcliffe Hall as the battalion's new headquarters and drill hall (see Chapter 6). In 1924, in recognition of their services, the battalion was retitled as simply the Hallamshire Battalion, and in so doing, making it one of very few territorial units in Britain not to be known by a number.

In May 1939, the battalion attained the war establishment of 31 officers and 630 other ranks. As war on the continent threatened, a second line battalion was formed and titled the 6th Battalion, the York and Lancaster Regiment. Early in the Second World War, the Hallamshires were deployed to Norway, before being moved to Iceland where they remained for two years.

The battalion then arrived in Normandy in June 1944, a few days after D-Day. The men saw action at Caen, le Havre, Antwerp, Venlo, Nijmegen and Arnhem (see Chapter 3). The

The Hallamshires on parade, 1911.

The 7th Battalion, York and Lancashire Regiment, First World War.

Hallamshires sustained 847 casualties during the war, while earning 27 awards, including a posthumous Victoria Cross to Corporal John William Harper (see Chapter 7).

The battalion broke from tradition in 1958 when, for the first time, a company was raised outside Sheffield at Rotherham. Three years later, a TA re-organization saw the Royal Artillery Battery at Barnsley, a direct descendent of the 5th Battalion, York and Lancaster Regiment, converted to infantry as a company of the Hallamshires.

First World War

In the war, the York and Lancaster Regiment contributed twenty-two battalions, earning fifty-nine battle honours – more than any other regiment. In addition to the 4th Hallamshires, Sheffield raised two territorial battalions: the 2/4th and the 12th (City of Sheffield).

Second World War

The regiment had ten battalions serve during the Second World War, earning fifty-five battle honours. The battalions and affiliate units were the 1st, 2nd, Hallamshires (TA), 6th (TA), 7th, 8th, 9th, 11th (Home), 67th (York and Lancaster) (H) A.A. Regiment, Royal Artillery (TA), and 150th Regiment, the Royal Armoured Corps (York and Lancaster).

The Queen's Own Yorkshire Dragoons

The Queen's Own Yorkshire Dragoons (QOYD) was a yeomanry regiment of the British Army in existence from 1794 to 1956. First raised as the South West Yorkshire Yeomanry Cavalry, in 1844 it was retitled the First West Yorkshire Yeomanry Cavalry. In May 1897, after the Sheffield squadron had the honour of escorting Her Majesty, Queen Victoria, at Sheffield, the regiment became known as the Queen's Own Yorkshire Dragoons.

Following major reversals during the so-called Black Week in South Africa, the regiment supplied three companies to serve in the Anglo-Boer War in 1900.

In the First World War, the 1/QOYD was deployed to France in July 1915. A Squadron from Sheffield came under the 17th (Northern) Division. The regiment's squadrons reassembled a year later to become corps cavalry to II Corps. In November 1917, it was transferred to the Cavalry Corps, where the only mounted action the regiment saw was in April 1917 when the Germans retreated to the Hindenburg Line. At the battles of the Somme (1916), the Ancre (1917) and Ypres (1917), the regiment provided infantry advances with Hotchkiss machine-gun support. At the Battle of Cambrai in 1917, the regiment became one of only six yeomanry regiments to serve in a regular cavalry division.

In February 1918, the men were converted to cyclists in II Corps. Demobilization of the regiment took place in July 1919.

During the inter-war years, only eight of the thirty-eight cavalry regiments remained mounted. The rest converted to armoured cars, signals, infantry and brigades of the Royal Field Artillery, while two were disbanded. The QOYD was one of the eight cavalry regiments to be retained.

In the Second World War, the QOYD was deployed in the Middle East theatre, where they saw action in the Lebanon and Syria. In February 1942, the QOYD was dismounted, becoming the last cavalry regiment in the British army. The regiment then converted to an armoured unit in North Africa, fighting in the Battle of Gazala and the First Battle of El Alamein.

Following major losses of armour in the Western Desert, the QOYD was issued with Bren carriers, 3in. mortars and 6pdr anti-tank guns and moved to the 2nd Armoured Brigade.

THE QUEEN AT SHEFFIELD

The Queen visited Sheffield on Friday for the purpose of opening the new Town Hall, when all the great workshops were idle and the usually grimy streets were resplendent with gaily-coloured bunting.

The Royal train, which left Windsor in the morning en route for Ballater, arrived at Sheffield at 5 o'clock, and was received with a Royal salute of 21 guns fired by a battery of the 4th West York Artillery Volunteers. A guard of honour of the Connaught Rangers was in attendance at the station, and the bands of the regiments enlivened the proceedings with some appropriate music.

The appearance of the Queen in the streets, lined with troops, and with military bands stationed at intervals, evoked a great outburst of enthusiasm.

Kirkintilloch Herald, Wednesday, 26 May 1897

Light Dragoons
and Queen's
Own Yeomanry
on exercises
in Morocco.
(Photo MoD)

Towards the end of October 1942, the regiment sustained major casualties during the Second Battle of Al Alamein when they became bogged down in the congested minefields.

During the next eight months of its deployment in North Africa, the regiment was again converted, this time to 'lorried' infantry and retitled the 9th (Yorkshire Dragoons) Battalion, King's Own Yorkshire Light Infantry, as part of 18th (Lorried) Infantry Brigade.

In February 1944, now with the 1st Infantry Division under the US Fifth Army, the battalion then participated in the Italian campaign, pushing the German army northwards. On 13 March, the regiment sustained 170 casualties, which were not replaced. Consequently, in August, the original members of the regiment were repatriated home.

After the war, Yorkshire's yeomanry regiments amalgamated as the Queen's Own Yorkshire Yeomanry, formed in April 1967 as a TAVR III unit. In April 1971, the regiment was re-formed once more, becoming A Squadron, the Queen's Own Yeomanry.

Sheffield University Officers' Training Corps (SUOTC)

In 1900, the University of Sheffield, with War Office endorsement, raised a company titled G Company, the West Yorkshire Royal Engineers. In 1911, Sheffield University raised an Officers' Training Corps contingent. One of its former members, Lieutenant William Allen, earned the Victoria Cross on the Western Front during the First World War (see Chapter 7).

In September 2011, Sheffield and Leeds University Officers' Training Corps were brought together under the Yorkshire Officers' Training Regiment (YOTR), catering for students from universities across Yorkshire.

The Sheffield University Officers' Training Corps (SUOTC) is one the largest in the country, serving the University of Sheffield and Sheffield Hallam University. The SUOTC is based at Somme Barracks in the Sheffield city centre.

6. BARRACKS AND BUILDINGS

Hillsborough Barracks

In February 1851, Pickard and Ogden invited tenders for 'the erection of the new barracks, at Owlerton, near Sheffield'. On Wednesday, 11 October 1854, five companies of the 2nd West York West York Light Infantry arrived in Sheffield from the regimental barracks in York. The 'clean, steady, soldier-like' troops marched through the town to take up residence in the new barracks.

Constructed more along the lines of a castle, the barracks was among the largest in Britain. With added Gothic-style architecture, the sprawling 22-acre site has stone perimeter walls up to 4ft wide, with turrets at every corner.

Erected originally as a garrison for horse and foot regiments, the first phase of construction included a chapel, hospital, parade square, stables, farrier's shop, veterinary hospital and riding school. In the period up to the turn of the century, there were further additions, including married quarters, rifle range, gymnasium, vehicle workshops and an infants' school, and by 1889, the military cantonment was being called Hillsborough Barracks. What is interesting to note, is that living quarters were fronted with verandas, a feature more associated with the much warmer climes of places like India.

Hillsborough Barracks. (Photo Chemical Engineer)

BALAKLAVA, OCTOBER 27TH, 1854

My Lord – I have the honour to report that the cavalry division under my command was seriously engaged with the enemy on the 25th instant, during the greater part of which day it was under a heavy fire; that it made a most triumphant charge against a very superior number of the enemy's cavalry, and an attack upon batteries which for daring and gallantry could not be exceeded. The loss, however, in officers, men, and horses, has been most severe.

The heavy brigade had soon to return to the support of the troops defending Balaklava, and was fortunate in being at hand when a large force of Russian cavalry was descending the hill. I immediately ordered Brigadier-General Scarlett to attack with his Scots Greys and Enniskillen Dragoons, and had his attack supported in second line by the Fifth Dragoon Guards, and by a flank attack of the Fourth Dragoon Guards.

Under every disadvantage of ground, these eight small squadrons succeeded in defeating and dispersing a body of cavalry estimated at three times their number and more.

The attack of the light cavalry was very brilliant and daring; exposed to a fire from heavy batteries on their front and two flanks, they advanced unchecked until they reached the batteries of the enemy, and cleared them of their gunners, and only retired when they found themselves engaged with a very superior force of cavalry in the rear. Major-General the Earl of Cardigan led this attack in the most gallant and intrepid manner; and his lordship has expressed himself to me as admiring in the highest degree the courage and zeal of every officer, non-commissioned officer, and man that assisted.

The losses, my Lord, it grieves me to state, have been very great indeed, and, I fear will be much felt by your Lordship.

I have, &c.,

LUCAN, Lieutenant-General, Commanding Cavalry Division.

Leeds Intelligencer, Saturday, 18 November 1854

On their return from the Crimea in 1856, the 4th (Royal Irish) Dragoon Guards were quartered at the barracks. At this time, the 98th (Prince of Wales's) Regiment of Foot was also based at Hillsborough. In September 1857, at the barracks, Lieutenant General James Thomas Brudenell, 7th Earl of Cardigan KCB, and the man who led the infamous charge of the Light Brigade in the Crimean campaign, inspected a parade of the 7th (The Princess Royal's) Dragoon Guards prior to their departure for a tour of duty in India.

In the 1870s through to 1897, Hillsborough Barracks was also home to batteries of the Royal Artillery and the Royal Horse Artillery. From 1897, for a brief four-year interlude, Hillsborough ceased to house artillery units and returned to housing the cavalry, with

A Squadron, 2nd Dragoon Guards (Queen's Bays) taking up residence. The squadron moved out in 1899, and in 1901, the 32nd Brigade, Royal Field Artillery, returned.

During the war in South Africa, elements of the volunteer Yorkshire Dragoons and the Yorkshire Hussars were trained at Hillsborough in 1900.

These are the military units known to have been based at the barracks:

2nd West York West York Light Infantry, 1854
4th Royal Irish Dragoon Guards, 1856
98th (Prince of Wales's) Regiment of Foot, 1856
7th (Princess Royal's) Dragoon Guards, 1857
24th (Warwickshire) Regiment of Foot, 1859
58th (Rutlandshire) Regiment of Foot, 1861
16th (Bedfordshire) Regiment of Foot, 1861
22nd (Cheshire) Regiment of Foot, 1870
E Battery, Royal Horse Artillery, 1870s
A Squadron, 2nd Dragoon Guards (Queen's Bays), 1897
6th Battalion (Louth Militia), the Royal Irish Rifles, 1899
Yorkshire Dragoons and Yorkshire Hussars, training for the Anglo-Boer War, 1900
32nd Brigade, Royal Field Artillery, 1901
2nd Battalion, the King's Own Yorkshire Light Infantry, 1905
2nd Battalion, the Cheshire Regiment, 1920
29th Field (Howitzer) Battery, vacating the barracks in February 1930

In the late 1980s, a major redevelopment of the barracks saw the site converted in a large retail park, while the former hospital building became part of Sheffield College.

The barracks enjoys Grade II listed status.

Norfolk Barracks

Situated on Clough Road, construction of the Norfolk Barracks commenced on 25 September 1878, when Flora Fitzalan-Howard, 15th Duchess of Norfolk, laid the foundation stone. The property of the West Riding of Yorks County Association, the complex, erected at a cost of £13,000, was officially opened on 2 June 1880. The drill hall would be for the 4th West York Artillery Volunteers, which gave rise to confusion about both the name and the address of the buildings. The association named it the Volunteer Artillery Drill Hall, Edmund Road, whereas it was more officially known as Norfolk Barracks, in recognition of the generous £5,000 contribution towards the construction from Henry Fitzalan-Howard, the 15th Duke of Norfolk. The barracks faces on to Clough Road.

Designed by architects Messrs M. E. Hadfield & Son, the barracks comprised a main hall, measuring 180ft by 90ft, which was constructed with a single-span roof with no pillar supports. Primarily intended for drill, the hall, with a capacity of 12,000 to 2,500 seated – was well-suited for concerts, balls and public meetings. Attached to the hall, there

Norfolk Barracks, also known as the Volunteer Artillery Drill Hall. (Photo Warofdreams)

was a gun-shed equal in length, but narrower. In addition to a riding school, there were also stables and harness rooms. Above the main entrance, a recess in the square tower displays the armorial bearings of the Howard family, and the motto 'Sola Virtus Invicta' – bravery alone is invincible.

The occupants were given as 7, 8 and 9 batteries of the 3rd, West Riding Brigade, Royal Field Artillery. The units were equipped with Ordnance 15-pounder BLC (breech loading converted) light field guns.

Typical of drill halls of the period, the building was largely a venue for a wide range of social and community activities: dances, commercial and trade exhibitions, sporting events and flower shows. In 1903, Prime Minister Arthur Balfour addressed a political meeting in the hall, and in another political gathering three years later, members of the suffragettes' movement ruined the meeting.

From 1906 to 1912, Secretary of War, Richard Haldane, introduced a major re-organization of the British army. In 1908, yeomanry and volunteer regiments were merged into a territorial army, comprising fourteen infantry divisions and fourteen cavalry brigades. In 1912, in pursuance of the national exercise, Norfolk Barracks became Crown property. The building was closed for refurbishment, and re-opened by Chief of the Imperial General Staff Sir John French on 24 May 1912.

In 1979, mobility specialists Clark & Partners acquired the property. In April 2005, it was sold by auction for £1.1 million. In 2011, the building was converted into luxury apartments.

Somme Barracks

Situated on the corner of Glossop Road and Gell Street, the past purpose of the brick building can be recognized by the legend '1st W.Y.R.E. (Vols)' – the 1st West Yorkshire Royal Engineers – the home of the West Riding Divisional Royal Engineers. The wall also carries the royal coat of arms and, above that and in between two multi-sided turrets, the date '1907'.

In 1882, the 1st West York Engineer Volunteers moved from their existing headquarters on John Street in the Sheffield suburb of Highfield, to a spacious house adjoining the site of the future barracks. In July 1906, commanding officer Lieutenant Colonel Edward Tozer launched an appeal for funds to erect the new headquarters. Architect Alfred Turnell, who was also corps quartermaster, was tasked with the design work. The land was purchased for £3,000 and the cost of construction came to £6,500.

The red-brick and ashlar-stone-dressed Renaissance-style building is L-shaped and has two storeys. On the Glossop Road external wall, there is a First World War memorial plaque to members of the corps. The new facility included offices for the commanding officer and the adjutant, a large armoury and dedicated workshop, a surgery, a canteen, and orderly and lecture rooms.

The General Officer Commanding-in-Chief for Northern Command, General Sir Laurence James Oliphant KCB, KCVO, 9th of Condie and 31st Chief of Clan Oliphant, opened the barracks on 7 December 1907.

Somme Barracks, with inset of the memorial plaque. (Photos Gerry van Tonder)

OBITUARY

Colonel Edward Sanderson Tozer, of the Chestnuts, Westbourne Road, Sheffield, died at his residence yesterday at noon after a long period of unsatisfactory health.

He was born at Sheffield in 1857, his father being the late Mr. Edward Tozer, a steel manufacturer, who held the position of Mayor in 1880–81, and of Master Cutler for two years – 1875 and 1876. Finishing his education at St. Peter's School, York, the deceased entered the well-known firm of Steed, Peech, and Tozer.

Colonel Tozer did not aspire to public life, and apart from business he found his chief interest in Volunteer work. He joined the 1st West York Royal Engineer Volunteers in 1879, and in 1900 assumed command. He received the Volunteer officers' decoration in 1899. He was also a vice-president of the Yorkshire Rifle Association. He was a prominent Freemason, a Churchman, and a Conservative.

Yorkshire Post and *Leeds Intelligencer*, Monday, 9 December 1907

The West York Royal Engineers tenure was, however, short lived. In April the following year, the new Territorial and Reserve Forces Act 1907, brainchild of Richard Haldane, saw the War Office acquiring the building at a fraction of its value. In 1910, men of the corps financed the erection of a covered riding school at the barracks.

At the outbreak of the First World War, the corps was formed into the 1st (West Riding) Field Company, Divisional Royal Engineers, under the command of Lieutenant Colonel Sir Albert E. Bingham. The unit saw action in the Beaumont Hamel sector at the Battle of the Somme in 1916, by this time retitled the 455th (West Riding) Field Company, Royal Engineers, and part of the 29th Division. The barracks was named in remembrance of this.

At various times, the 2nd (West Riding) Field Company, Royal Engineers, and the West Riding Divisional Telegraph Company were also stationed at the Somme Barracks.

Until the 1990s, the barracks was the headquarters of both the 106 (West Riding) Field Squadron (Volunteers) and the University of Sheffield Officer Training Corps (OTC). The field squadron relocated to the new Bailey Barracks at Greenhill, Sheffield, in 1994 leaving the University OTC as the only military resident until, more recently, the Sheffield Detachment, Burma Company, the 4th Battalion, the Yorkshire Regiment, took up occupation of part of the building. Now the city's Army Reserve Centre, the building also houses the Territorial Auxiliary and Volunteer Reserve Association.

Endcliffe Hall

Formed in May 1859, the Hallamshire Rifle Volunteers established their headquarters at what was referred to as 'the Depot in Eyre Street', while conducting drills at the Collegiate School and Bramall Lane cricket ground.

Endcliffe Hall.

Following the 1881 reforms of the British army, the now titled 1st (Hallamshire) Volunteer Battalion, the York and Lancaster Regiment, moved to Hyde Park Barracks, on former recreation grounds in St John's Road, over Easter 1886. In 1908, the unit was redesignated the 4th (Hallamshire) Battalion, the York and Lancaster Regiment (TF), and in 1914, new headquarters were established at Endcliffe Hall.

Situated in 'one of the most delightful parts of Sheffield', Endcliffe Hall was constructed in 1862 by local steel magnate Sir John Brown, with architects Flockton & Abbot doing the design work. Costing the wealthy Brown £100,000, it is the largest private residence in Sheffield. The double-storey hall was built in the Italianate style with stone ashlar dressing. A three-storey, square Belvedere tower bisects the main west-facing façade.

Following the death of his wife in 1881, the distraught Brown spent less and less time at Endcliffe Hall, eventually selling the magnificent property in 1895 for a paltry £26,000 to property developers Barber Bros. & Wortley. Brown died the following year. The consortium failed to capitalize on their investment, however, and the building hosted a miscellany of public events.

Eventually, the hall stood empty and was in danger of being pulled down, until former Hallamshires' commanding officer and mayor of Sheffield, Colonel George Ernest Branson, purchased the building, believing it would make 'splendid headquarters for the regiment'. Government subsequently acquired the property, and work started on refurbishment to enable the regiment to take up residence after their 1914 summer camp.

Included in the adaptation of the hall to purpose, the stables were converted into an armoury, wagon, gun and storage sheds, and an orderly room. The hall accommodated billiards and recreation rooms, as well as the sergeants' mess and officers' quarters. A new drill hall was erected in the expansive grounds.

Endcliffe Hall was to remain the headquarters of the Hallamshires until the unit was disbanded in 1968. Today, the Grade II-listed property is the base for the Sheffield detachment of the 4th Battalion, Yorkshire Regiment (TA Reserve) and the 212 (Yorkshire) Field Hospital. The whole estate is still a military reserve, with restricted public access as those stationed there are on constant anti-terrorist standby.

St George's Regimental Chapel

The original, small regimental chapel to the York and Lancaster Regiment in the Sheffield Cathedral was dedicated on 14 February 1939 as a memorial to the city's most illustrious son, Field Marshal Viscount Herbert Onslow Plumer of Messines, who died on 16 July 1932 and is buried in Westminster Abbey.

Following post-war alterations to the cathedral, St George's Chapel was initially intended to be the new sanctuary. On 15 November 1966, in the presence of Princess Margaret, sister to the Queen, the Bishop of Sheffield consecrated the new chapel, which was adopted by the regiment on 22 April 1967.

At the entrance to the chapel off the nave, a white stone memorial set in the floor carries a brass inscription, 'Dedicated to the Memory of all ranks of the York and Lancaster

St George's Regimental Chapel, Sheffield Cathedral. (Photo Oosoom)

Regiment who have given their lives for their country and in the service of the Regiment since its formation in 1758'.

Numerous memorials are found throughout the chapel. Among the small stained-glass windows, is one that depicts the types of decorations awarded to the regiment's brave: the Victoria Cross, Distinguished Service Order, Military Cross, Distinguished Conduct Medal and the Military Medal. A further four windows display landmark events in the regiment's history: Salonika, Burma, Europe and Suvla Bay, Gallipoli.

Below the ceiling hang the 2nd Battalion King's and Regimental Colours 1927–47, the 1st Battalion Queen's and Regimental Colours 1957–68, and the 1st Battalion Coldstream Guards King's and Regimental Colours.

A unique feature on the right side of the chapel is a memorial screen made up of swords and bayonets. Presented by the York and Lancaster Regiment on its disbandment in 1968, the swords point up, symbolic of the regiment's readiness to serve, while the bayonets point down, signifying the laying down of weapons of war.

Above the screen, there is another rank of regimental and monarch's colours: 1st Battalion 1905–22, 2nd Battalion 1891–1927, Hallamshire Rifles 1862–1908, and the First World War service battalions, the 2/4th Hallamshires, and the 6th, 7th, 9th, 10th and 12th.

7. FOR VALOUR

Awarded for 'most conspicuous bravery, or some daring or pre-eminent act of valour or self-sacrifice, or extreme devotion to duty in the presence of the enemy', the Victoria Cross, since its institution in 1856, is Britain's highest gallantry award, with precedence over all other medals and awards. These are the recipients from the York and Lancaster and antecedent regiments.

Captain William Barnsley Allen, MB

Royal Army Medical Corps (RAMC)
Victoria Cross citation, London Gazette, 26 October 1916

For most conspicuous bravery and devotion to duty.

When gun detachments were unloading H.E. ammunition from wagons which had just come up, the enemy suddenly began to shell the battery position. The first shell fell on one of the limbers, exploded the ammunition and caused several casualties.

Captain Allen saw the occurrence and at once, with utter disregard of danger, ran straight across the open, under heavy shell fire, commenced dressing the wounded, and undoubtedly by his promptness saved many of them from bleeding to death.

He was himself hit four times during the first hour by pieces of shells, one of which fractured two of his ribs, but he never even mentioned this at the time, and coolly went on with his work till the last man was dressed and safely removed.

The Victoria Cross. (Photo MoD)

He then went over to another battery and tended a wounded officer. It was only when this was done that he returned to his dug-out and reported his own injury.

Distinguished Service Order citation, London Gazette, 10 December 1919:
Captain (A/Major) William Barnsley Allen, VC, MC, MB
RAMC, attached l/3rd (West Riding) Field Ambulance

For conspicuous gallantry and devotion to duty during the fighting west of Saulzoir for the Selle River line between the 11th and 14th October, 1918. He showed a very high degree of fearless initiative in organising the collection of wounded from ground under continuous hostile shell fire, and by his inspiring example, untiring energy and contempt of danger, he was able to move large numbers of helpless wounded from positions of danger before he was himself gassed.

Bar to the Military Cross, London Gazette, 26 September 1916:
Captain William Barnsley Allen VC, MC
R.A.M.C.

   For conspicuous gallantry and devotion to duty. During an intense bombardment of a town with high explosive and gas shells, he left the Advance Dressing Station to search for wounded men. Hearing that there were some in a remote part of the town, he proceeded there, collected them, and supervised their removal to the Dressing Station. On his return, hearing that a party under another Officer had not come in, he was on the point of starting out again to look, for them when they appeared. Although seriously gassed, he continued to perform his duties with the greatest devotion and gallantry, until eventually evacuated to the Casualty Clearing Station.

Military Cross citation, London Gazette, 26 September 1916:
Captain William Barnsley Allen, MB
R.A.M.C.

   For conspicuous gallantry and devotion to duty. He was telephoned for when an artilleryman was severely wounded, and came in at once over ground which was being heavily shelled at the time. On another occasion he did similar fine work under heavy shell fire.

Lance Corporal Abraham Boulger VC. (Photo IWM)

Lance Corporal Abraham Boulger

84th Regiment of Foot
Victoria Cross citation, London Gazette, 18 June 1858:

   For distinguished bravery and forwardness; as a skirmisher, in all the twelve actions fought between 12th July, and 25th September, 1857. (Extract from Field Force Orders of the late Major-General Havelock, dated 17th October, 1857.)

Private John Caffrey

2nd Battalion, York and Lancaster Regiment
Victoria Cross citation, London Gazette, 21 January 1916:

   For most conspicuous bravery on 16th November, 1915, near La Brique. A man of the West Yorkshire Regiment had been badly wounded and was lying in the open unable to move in full view of and about 300 to 400 yards from the enemy's trenches. Corporal Stirk, Royal Army Medical Corps, and Private Caffrey at once started out to rescue him, but at the first attempt they were driven back by shrapnel fire. Soon afterwards they started again under close sniping and machine-gun fire, and succeeded in reaching and bandaging the wounded man. but, just as Corporal Stirk had lifted him on Private Caffrey's back, he himself was shot in the head.

Private Caffrey put down the wounded man, bandaged Corporal Stirk and helped him back into safety. He then returned and brought in the man of the West Yorkshire Regiment. He had made three journeys across the open under close and accurate fire and had risked his own life to save others with the utmost coolness and bravery.

Acting Sergeant John Brunton Daykins

2/4th (Hallamshire) Battalion, York and Lancaster Regiment
Victoria Cross citation, Edinburgh Gazette, 10 January 1919:

For most conspicuous bravery and initiative at Solésmes on 20th October 1918, when, with twelve remaining men of his platoon, he worked his way most skilfully, in face of heavy opposition, towards the church. By prompt action he enabled his party to rush a machine gun, and during subsequent severe hand-to-hand fighting he himself disposed of many of the enemy and secured his objective, his party, in addition to heavy casualties inflicted, taking thirty prisoners.

He then located another machine gun which was holding up a portion of his company. Under heavy fire he worked his way alone to the post, and shortly afterwards returned with twenty-five prisoners and an enemy machine gun, which he mounted at his post.

His magnificent fighting spirit and example inspired his men, saved many casualties, and contributed very largely to the success of the attack.

Corporal John William Harper (Posthumous)

4th (Hallamshire) Battalion, York and Lancaster Regiment
Victoria Cross citation, London Gazette, 2 January 1945:
The KING has been graciously pleased to approve the posthumous award of the VICTORIA CROSS to:

No. 4751678 Corporal John William Harper, The York and Lancaster Regiment (Doncaster). In North-West Europe, on 29th September, 1944, the Hallamshire Battalion of the York and Lancaster Regiment attacked the Depot de Mendicite, a natural defensive position surrounded by an earthen wall, and then a dyke, strongly held by the enemy.

Corporal Harper was commanding the leading section in the assault. The enemy were well dug in and had a perfect field of fire across 300 yards of completely flat and exposed country. With superb disregard for the hail of mortar bombs and small arms fire which the enemy brought to bear on this open ground, Corporal Harper led his section straight up to the wall and killed or captured the enemy holding the near side.

During this operation, the platoon commander was seriously wounded and Corporal Harper took over control of the platoon.

As the enemy on the far side of the wall were now throwing grenades over the top, Corporal Harper climbed over the wall alone, throwing grenades, and in the face of heavy, close range small arms fire, personally routed the Germans directly opposing him. He took four prisoners and shot several of the remainder of the enemy as they fled.

Still completely ignoring the heavy spandau [machine gun] and mortar fire, which was sweeping the area, once again he crossed the wall alone to find out whether it was possible for his platoon to wade the dyke which lay beyond. He found the dyke too deep and wide to cross, and once again he came back over the wall and received orders to try and establish his platoon on the enemy side of it. For the third time he climbed over alone, found some empty German weapon pits, and providing the covering fire urged and encouraged his section to scale the wall and dash for cover. By this action he was able to bring down sufficient covering fire to enable the rest of the company to cross the open ground and surmount the wall for the loss of only one man.

Corporal Harper then left his platoon in charge of his senior section commander and walked alone along the banks of the dyke, in the face of heavy spandau fire, to find a crossing place. Eventually he made contact with the battalion attacking on his right, and found that they had located a ford. Back he came across the open ground, and, whilst directing his company commander to the ford, he was struck by a bullet which fatally wounded him and he died on the bank of the dyke.

The success of the battalion in driving the enemy from the wall and back across the dyke must be largely ascribed to the superb self sacrifice and inspiring gallantry of Corporal Harper. His magnificent courage, fearlessness and devotion to duty throughout the battle set a splendid example to his men and had a decisive effect on the course of the operations.

Private Joel Holmes

84th Regiment of Foot

Victoria Cross citation, London Gazette, 18 June 1858:

For distinguished conduct in volunteering to assist in working a gun of Captain Maude's Battery, under a heavy fire, from which gun nearly all the Artillerymen had been shot away. (Extract from Field Force Orders of the late Major-General Havelock, dated 17th October, 1857.)

Sergeant Major George Lambert

84th Regiment of Foot

Victoria Cross citation, London Gazette, 18 June 1858:

For distinguished conduct, at Onao, on the 29th of July; at Bithoor, on the 16th of August; and at Lucknow, on the 25th of September. (Extract from Field Force Orders of the late Major-General Havelock, dated 17th October, 1857.)

Sergeant Frederick Charles Riggs (Posthumous)

6th Battalion, York and Lancaster Regiment

Victoria Cross citation, Edinburgh Gazette, 10 January 1919:

For most conspicuous bravery and self sacrifice on the morning of the 1st October 1918, near Epinoy, when, having led his platoon through strong uncut wire under severe fire, *he continued straight on, and, although losing heavily from flanking fire, succeeded in reaching his objective, where he rushed and captured a machine gun.*

He later handled two captured guns with great effect, and caused the surrender of fifty enemy.

Subsequently, when the enemy again advanced in force, Sjt. Riggs cheerfully encouraged his men to resist, and whilst exhorting his men to fight on to the last, this very gallant soldier was killed.

Lance Corporal John Ryan (see Chapter 3)
65th Regiment of Foot
Victoria Cross citation, London Gazette, 18 June 1858:
For gallant conduct at the engagement near Cameron-town above referred to. This Non-Commissioned Officer, with Privates Bulford and Talbot [both awarded the Distinguished Conduct Medal], of the same Regiment, who have been recommended for the Medal for distinguished conduct in the Field, for their behaviour on the same occasion, removed the body of the late Captain Swift from the Field of Action, after he had been mortally wounded, and remained with it all night in a bush surrounded by the enemy.

Lance Corporal John Sinnott
84th Regiment of Foot
Victoria Cross citation, Edinburgh Gazette, 28 December 1858:
For conspicuous gallantry at Lucknow, on the 6th of October 1857, in going out with Serjeants Glinn and Mullins, and Private Mullins, to rescue Lieutenant Gibaut, who, in carrying out water to extinguish a fire in the breastwork, had been mortally wounded, and lay outside. They brought in the body under a heavy fire. Lance-Corporal Sinnott was twice wounded. His comrades unanimously elected him for the Victoria Cross, as the most worthy.

He had previously repeatedly accompanied Lieutenant Gibaut when he carried out water to extinguish the fire. (Despatch from Lieutenant-General Sir James Out ram, Bart., G.C.B., dated 2d December 1857.)

Captain The Honourable Augustus Henry Archibald Anson
84th Regiment of Foot
Victoria Cross citation, Edinburgh Gazette, 28 December 1858:
For conspicuous bravery at Bolundshahur, on the 28th September 1857. The 9th Light Dragoons had charged through the town, and were re-forming in the Serai; the enemy attempted to close the entrance by drawing their carts across it, so as to shut in the cavalry and form a cover from which to fire upon them. Captain Anson, taking a lance, dallied out of the gateway, and knocked the drivers off their carts. Owing to a wound in his left hand, received at Delhi, he could not stop his horse, and rode into the middle of the enemy, who fired a volley at him, one ball passing through his coat. At Lucknow, at the assault of the Secundra Bagh, on 16th November 1857, he entered with the storming party, on the gates being burst open. He had his horse killed, and was himself slightly wounded. He has shewn

the greatest gallantry on every occasion, and has slain many enemies in fight. (Despatch from Major-General Sir James Hope Grant, K.C.B., dated 12th August 1858.)

Private Samuel Harvey
1st Battalion, The York and Lancaster Regiment
Victoria Cross citation, London Gazette, 18 November 1915:

For most conspicuous bravery in "Big Willie" trench on 29th September, 1915.

During a heavy bombing attack by the enemy, and when more bombs were urgently required for our front, Private Harvey volunteered to fetch them. The communication trench was blocked with wounded and reinforcements, and he went backwards and forwards across the open under intense fire and succeeded in bringing up no less than thirty boxes of bombs before he was wounded in the head. It was mainly due to Private Harvey's cool bravery in supplying bombs that the enemy was eventually driven back.

Colour Sergeant Edward McKenna (see Chapter 3)
65th Regiment of Foot
Victoria Cross citation, London Gazette, 18 June 1858:

For gallant conduct at the engagement near Cameron-town, New Zealand, on the 7th of September, 1863, after both his officers, Captain Swift and Lieutenant Butler, had been shot, in charging through the position of an enemy heavily outnumbering him, and drawing off his small force, consisting of two Serjeants, one bugler, and thirty-five men, through a broken and rugged country, with the loss of but one man killed, and another missing.

Lieutenant General Cameron, C.B., Commanding Her Majesty's Forces in that colony, reports that, in Colour-Serjeant MacKenna, the detachment found a Commander whose coolness, intrepidity, and judgment, justified the confidence placed in him by the soldiers brought so suddenly under his command.

Private Patrick Mylott
84th Regiment of Foot
Victoria Cross citation, Edinburgh Gazette, 28 December 1858:

For being foremost in rushing across a road, under a shower of balls, to take an opposite enclosure; and for gallant conduct at every engagement at which he was present with his Regiment, from 12th of July 1857 to the relief of the garrison. (Elected by the private soldiers of the Regiment.)

Colour Sergeant Edward McKenna VC. (Photo Auckland Museum)

8. LEST WE FORGET

A commemorative tribute in pictures.

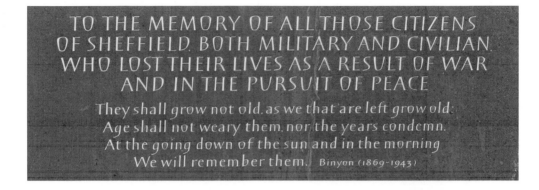

Above: Plaque in the Peace Gardens, Sheffield.
(Photo Gerry van Tonder)

Right: Sheffield War Memorial.
(Photo Gerry van Tonder)

Bronze Boer War Memorial, Weston Park, Sheffield. (Photo Gerry van Tonder)

York and Lancaster Regiment War Memorial plinth, Weston Park, Sheffield. (Photo Gerry van Tonder)

The York and Lancaster Regiment War Memorial, Weston Park, Sheffield. (Photo Gerry van Tonder)

Above: Serre Road Cemetery No. 2, Somme, France. (Photo CWGC)

Left: Hollinsend War Memorial. (Photo Mick Knapton)

Norton War Memorial. (Photo Warofdreams)

> ## SPANISH CIVIL WAR 1936-1939
> IN HONOUR OF THE SOUTH YORKSHIRE MEN WHO FOUGHT ALONGSIDE THE SPANISH PEOPLE IN THEIR STRUGGLE FOR DEMOCRACY AND OF THE LOCAL MEN AND WOMEN WHO WORKED IN SUPPORT OF THE CAUSE
> ### THESE DIED IN SPAIN
> M. AARONBERG (JARAMA 2·37) G. ALLSTOP (EBRO 8·38)
> W. BRENT (EBRO 8·38) A. NEWSUM (CORDOVA 1·37)
> H. TAGG (JARAMA 2·37) F. TURNHILL (TERUEL 1·38)
> ### THESE ALSO FOUGHT IN SPAIN
> J. ALBAYA · A. COOPER · T. DEGNAN · T. JAMES · J. MAIDEN
> R. RYDER · C. SMITH · A. STIRLING · S. WARD · H. WINDLE
>
> Yet. Freedom yet. thy banner torn but flying
> Streams like a thunder storm against the wind
> BYRON

Above: Spanish Civil War Memorial plaque, Peace Gardens, Sheffield. (Photo Gerry van Tonder)

Left: Commonwealth War Graves Commission grave of Sergeant Alec Webster Oates from Sheffield, Harare Pioneer Cemetery, Zimbabwe. Died in an aircraft crash while undergoing RAF pilot training in Southern Rhodesia. (Photo Mike Tucker)

Owlerton War Memorial Hall. (Photo Mick Knapton)

Chapeltown War Memorial.
(Photo Martin Speck)

(Photo Gerry van Tonder)

SOURCES & ACKNOWLEDGEMENTS

As source material, these two Pen & Sword titles were particularly useful: Paul Oldfield's and Ralph Gibson's *Sheffield City Battalion: The 12th (Service) Battalion York and Lancaster Regiment: A History of the Battalion raised by Sheffield in World War One* (2016). and Geoffrey Powell's *Plumer: The Soldier's General* (2004).

I extend my sincere gratitude to John Nash of the Rotherham Museum, and local regimental historian, Jayne Daley. It was great sharing.

As always, special thanks to Colonel Dudley Wall for not only his outstanding graphics in the colour plates, but, more importantly, for his friendship and loyalty to our shared vision for the preservation of military history.

Thank you, Joanna Neal, for the most incredible original Boer War photos.

Particular thanks to a group of generous folk in New Zealand who went out of their way to source for me material on the 65th Regiment of Foot and the engagement at the Alexandra Redoubt: close friend in Tauranga, Hugh Bomford, who rallied everyone to assist, Charles Chapman of the Auckland War Memorial Museum, Bruce Cairns of the 65th Regiment of Foot Re-enactment Unit in Auckland, and Brian Griffiths for trekking through New Zealand countryside in search of Camerontown.

ABOUT THE AUTHOR

Born in Southern Rhodesia, now Zimbabwe, historian and author Gerry van Tonder came to Britain in 1999. Specializing in military history, Gerry has authored *Rhodesian Combined Forces Roll of Honour 1966–1981*; *Book of Remembrance: Rhodesia Native Regiment and Rhodesian African Rifles*; *North of the Red Line* (South African Defence Forces border war), and the co-authored definitive *Rhodesia Regiment 1899–1981*. Gerry presented a copy of the latter to the regiment's former colonel-in-chief, Her Majesty the Queen. He has also had published the first title in Pen & Sword's new Cold War series, *The Berlin Blockade: Soviet Chokehold and the Great Allied Airlift, 1948–49*, which was followed by *Malayan Emergency: Triumph of the Running Dogs, 1948–1960* and *North Korea Invades the South: Across the 38th Parallel, June 1950*, the first volume of six dealing with the Korean War. Gerry has also written on local history, including *Nottingham's Military Legacy*, *Derby in 50 Buildings*, *Chesterfield's Military Heritage* and *Mansfield through Time*.